Spell

BOOKS WITH ARTISTS

Thripsis
(with Joe Brainard)

A Clown, Some Colors, A Doll, Her Stories, A Song, A Moonlit Cove
(with Ellen Phelan)

How Things Bear Their Telling
(with Lucio Pozzi)

Greeks
(with Jan Groover and Bruce Boice)

Sacred Weather
(with Louisa Chase)

letters or syllables are given their usual sounds in situations rather than the sounds heard among speakers who make greatest use of the word \'wȯ(r)ˌsestə(r)\ instead of \'wu̇stə(r)\ for *Worcester*, or \'bōtˌswān\ instead of \'bōs°n\ for *boatswain* are spelling pronunciations)

spelling reform *n* : a movement to alter the conventional spellings so as to lessen or remove the inconsistencies in orthography and the pronunciation — compare REFORMED SPELLING

spelling school *n* : a spelling match esp. in the 19th century often serving as the social event of its day

spell out *vt* : to explain or state explicitly in clear terms 〈these views will be further spelled *out* —*Newsweek*〉 〈in a brief, seeming to *spell out* ... spelling anything *out* ... gets a ...〉

spells ...

1spelt \-lt\ ...akin to OHG *spaltan* to split; prob. fr. the splitting of the husk during threshing ...: a wheat (*Triticum spelta*) that is of no commercial importance ... its spikes with spikelets containing two ... called also *speltz*, compare EMMER

2spelt *chiefly Brit past of* SPELL

1spel·ter \'speltə(r)\ *n -s* [prob. modif. (influenced by It *peltro* pewter) of MD *speauter* spelter — more at PEWTER] **1** : ZINC *esp* : zinc cast in slabs for commercial use **2** : SPELTER SOLDER

2spelter \"\ *vt -ED/-ING/-S* : to solder with an alloy high in zinc ... made of three parts of zinc ... copper, iron, and brass ... : a variant in wheat having certain characteristics of spelt

speltz \'s(h)pelts\ *n -ES* [G *spelz* spelt, fr. OHG *spelza, spelta*, fr. LL *spelta* — more at SPELT] **1** : SPELT **2** : any of several varieties of emmer

spe·lun·car \spə'lᴐŋkər\ ... *-ar*] : of or relating to a cave

spe·lunk·er \"\ *n* ... + E *-er*; MF *spelunque*, fr. L *spelunca*, fr. Gk *spēlynx* — more at SPELEOLOGY] : one who makes a hobby of exploring and studying caves : CAVER — compare SPELEOLOGIST

spe·lunk·ing \-kiŋ\ *n -s* [obs. E *spelunk* cave + E *-ing*] : the hobby or practice of exploring caves

spence \'spen(t)s\ *n -s* [ME *spence, spense*, fr. MF *despense* place for storing supplies, supplies — more at DISPENSE] **1** *dial Brit* **a** : PANTRY **b** : CUPBOARD **2** *Scot* : an inner room usu. near the kitchen

1spen·cer \'spen(t)sə(r)\ *n -s* [after George John, 2d earl Spencer †1834 Eng. politician] **1 a** : a short double-breasted overcoat or jacket worn by men esp. in the 19th century **2** : a woman's fitted jacket of waist ... used abaft the foremast or the mainmast, hoisted upon a small supplementary mast, and set with a gaff and no boom **2** : a trysail abaft the foremast or mainmast

1spen·ce·ri·an \(')spen'sirēən, -ˌsēr-\ *adj, usu cap* [Herbert *Spencer* †1903 Eng. philosopher + E *-ian* (adj. suffix)] : of or relating to the philosopher Spencer or Spencerianism

2spencerian ... [Herbert *Spencer* †1903 + ... calligrapher the originator of the handwriting + E *-ian*] : of or characteristic of a form of slanting handwriting ... relating to or characteristic of a form of slanting handwriting

spen·cer cosmos ... of the operation of mechanical forces with the evolution of the cosmos from relative simplicity to relative complexity through the operation of mechanical forces with the acme of evolution being the equilibration of these forces after which dissolution begins and the cosmos goes back to the ultimate state from which evolution started

Spell

Ann Lauterbach

penguin poets

PENGUIN BOOKS
An imprint of Penguin Random House LLC
375 Hudson Street
New York, New York 10014
penguinrandomhouse.com

Acknowledgments to the original publishers of some of the poems in this book appear on page ix.

Excerpt from "Maximus to Gloucester, Letter 27 [withheld]" from *Selected Poems of Charles Olson*.
© 1997 by the Regents of the University of California. Published by the University of California Press

LIBRARY OF CONGRESS CATALOGING-IN-PUBLICATION DATA
Names: Lauterbach, Ann, — author.
Title: Spell / Ann Lauterbach.
Description: New York, New York : Penguin Books, [2018] | Series: Penguin poets
Identifiers: LCCN 2018017025 (print) | LCCN 2018018530 (ebook) |
ISBN 9780525505327 (ebook) | ISBN 9780143133520 (paperback)
Subjects: | BISAC: POETRY / American / General.
Classification: LCC PS3562.A844 (ebook) | LCC PS3562.A844 A6 2018 (print) |
DDC 811/.54—dc23
LC record available at https://lccn.loc.gov/2018017025

Printed in the United States of America
1 3 5 7 9 10 8 6 4 2

Set in Garamond MT Std
Designed by Ginger Legato

To JA

And then you sail past in your effortless bravado, the sky

a blue wind of ease, wings outstretched on a continuous

whim, as if there were no time, and there isn't,

but the rest of us pause, watching as you go, you go on by.

And for Anselm Berrigan and Nancy Shaver

ACKNOWLEDGMENTS

Some of these poems have appeared, often in earlier drafts, in print and online journals: *The American Reader, Bard Papers, Blackbox Manifold, Boston Review, The Brooklyn Rail, Conjunctions, Harper's, Literary Hub, The Poetry Foundation (Poem of the Day),* and *The Poetry Project Newsletter.* I wish to thank their editors, especially Brad Morrow, editor of *Conjunctions,* in which I have published work since 1981.

"Some of Us" was published originally in a book of photographs by Michael Carlebach (Asheville: Safe Harbor Books, 2017).

All etymologies are taken from the *Online Etymology Dictionary.*

I want also to convey deepest gratitude, once again, to my editor at Penguin, Paul Slovak, whose combination of patience, dedication, and responsiveness is extraordinary.

Many friends and colleagues have given me necessary buoyancy along the way. Among them: Arthur Gibbons, Michael Brenson, Marina van Zuylen, Michael Ives, Éric Trudel, Celia Bland, Thomas Wild, Anna Moschovakis, Roberto Tejada, and Peter Sweeny. Thank you.

Thank you to the ongoing assembly—students and faculty—of the Bard MFA for your beautiful commitment and conversation.

CONTENTS

The seen tree may be real enough for the sensation of vision, just as the dreamed tree is real enough for the dreamer as long as the dream lasts, but neither can ever become a real tree.

Hannah Arendt

Spell

PAUSE

The arc of distance is partial. A
continuum belated us, like the slow-motion
spit of a shaman. Friendships went south. We could not
name our freedoms, only the pause between days
in which all matters of belonging
densely accrued, then
scattered. I could not wake up. She wore
a tiara and spoke rapidly
into the swollen air,
youthful and eager, in bliss for that, while I
changed into a shadow just as the oil,
heating in the kitchen, began to snarl
and a single mosquito
itched against the screen, wanting
out, or blood. The arc of distance is partial.
The sun set into its given, not prone to regret or sorrow.

I'll stay in the thick jungle's weeds, without
expertise, and mystify the brand. A quotidian
logic animates the scene, heads
nodding, hands
busy under cover of night. I'll stay
here by the leaves yellowing in their
dotage, among sentences
dangling on webs and irreducible
to the temptation to flee. I'll
be here in the ancient shade of a crass
belligerent god, huge on a high wire,
teetering over an abyss. I'm here, sweetheart,
dressed in my skin, ready.

There is some kindness in the zone of farewell: handing
over the towel, removing the shoes, looking away
from the hanging figure's heavy pain,
sending a note: *Beloved, I regret*
you were not able to continue on this path
we made together, but did not follow,
and that your mouth fit so easily over its lies
like a kiss. No matter. We are
severed from the memorial's agenda,
which has, as you know,
moved on without us. The light is blue-gray
and the evidence of harm has been removed,
swept under the great litter they call *what happened.*

INVOCATION

Bring the huge vernacular.

Bring trysts of jealous

gods and a girl changed into a tree

and the tree, bring it

back or forward into

the foreseeable quantum dawn

shielding opalescent fog.

Bring days

by the road over which cats run

into the evening in diagonal cat shapes.

Please also to send Whitman's

ninety sorrowing words

from which to choose

as I do not, I

do not know

where the horizon is

located night or day to furnish

with cantilevered

messages from creatures

yet unnamed in the animate gusts

waiting for speech

that is *a wonder thing*.

OF THIS

And so traverses, gun in hand, the creek.
We on the other side waiting dreamily
as for a wave. The head of the tree
is heavy. The pears are not ripe.
I do not dare look up, seeing as
the day has splurged against my face
and you are on the other side
where the grid breaks into tiny, oracular
tiles, wafer thin, distorted.
The huge sound is mechanical, not
expressionistic: things
into other things, exploding.
The serial furthers. Were you
wearing a sombrero, or
just a hood to keep hot chords
from your skin? Serial, as in many
tunes, many kills, weeping
additions and accumulating, dry
remainders: the cost of endurance.

DESCENDANT

The claim's erasure darkens our
path, phrase by phrase; distance folds
onto jargon. Already
abstracted, an announcement
rises from the hoard of lesser-known trials,
as, from a burial site, a play.
Some plural; some assembly. Habitat
strewn with lyrics. Reception blank,
nothing to see in the choral chant.
The single episode was only another girl
walking along the beach, hair
woven with light, sandy toes wet,
there, on the far
island with its dunes, its grass.

Her wish is a form of shelter, the boys
having worn their jackets into
brambles, their hands
pierced and bleeding. Soon,
the shield and mirror will break
and all will cavort, naked, through
other, less tiring wars. The pilgrims
will turn back, cross the great waters
to the herald and the slain
calf, the thing with a diadem
in its illustrated hair.
The fictive largesse of theory's prize
lineated, then, by a thread of greenish force
but nothing spoken from the reflecting pool.
The family poses for a final portrait. They
each gaze, unsmiling, at the monumental lens.

SIGNAL, MOTIF

1.

They return to trade
places, they come back to play
among wet stones under
the fence along the path, to
fly out from sockets of air.
Not to imagine changes—
static to movement, gray to
rusted metallic—cropped
onto the brightly zoned
animate debris. To look,
to be held by a form
on the clock's deadpan face.
Just below artifice,
trillions again arguing for, or
molesting, the body's revision.

2.

O browned alley of restless

    leaves

        along the edge of sight

     there is nothing

to capture

    the halted yellow stick

        bow tied to tree

   stooped naked trunk

these

additions that amount to

selection

the way a vessel slides

yet unclosed if you happen to see

needles filtered

disclosed then

as if closer than light

disclosed as motion

whose scant repeat

over and under

knots the frame.

HERALD

Showing her hand *force quit*
showing template
threads across a mountain pass
hyped among syllables
stoned over the cusp of reason
looks down and across to find

how to pause   assemblage of sorrow   come
to change   fast architecture
sporting incognito   paint
impressions   held up
shields without consequence
acres of tiny sayings   iconographic kit
stripped of colors   redundant as sky

the margins swallowed
creatures on gold-plated spoons
code of signals
blurred as if distant
destiny's options sold to the girl with long legs
hurrying to catch a glimpse   fleeing the story.

FACT

—Hello, Evening.

—Hello. What's up?

—Just now a jet streamed across the sky, making a high, loud whine; my hands tingled with dread.

—It's a sound that causes alarm in many. Your experience on 9/11, living near Ground Zero, will always make this ripping roar one of terror for you. I have it, too, from time to time, with thunderstorms. It's as if all the beating hearts of the dead have gathered.

—Back when I read newspapers made of paper with news on them, I looked every day at the obituaries, and read many of them, not just the ones that detail the story of a life but those in tiny print, the names of the dead lined up next to each other in alphabetical order. How arbitrary it is, with whom your name appears; the company you keep in the alphabet of your dying day. Sharing the same death day is not something we think about, the way we think about sharing the same birthday.

—Well, that knowledge can't really be, can it, since your death day isn't known ahead of time. You will never know with whom you shared it. For a sentient human, you say some odd things.

—My neighbor around the corner has a sign on his lawn that reads "Jesus Died for Our Sins." I pass it each day.

—I'm glad I don't have to think about these kinds of beginnings and endings that cause such distress among you living. Nobody mourns me. I come and I go, I do not age, or get sick, or die.

—And yet you mark time, day after day. Sometimes, on the anniversary of a death of someone I once loved, I have felt as if that person's soul has entered and I become slowed and saturated, like a sponge. By now I know a lot of dead people and I realize that fewer and fewer among the living will have also known the people I knew— in a sense, still know.

—But knowing and remembering are not quite the same, or are they?

—Facts aren't the same as persons.

—But persons are facts, and you know and remember facts about them.

—But facts can never add up to a living being, which is why we grieve.

—Minds are so ornate! Language is so inadequate! I think you will be happier as a ghost.

—Maybe, although I do like being here. In dreams, the dead sometimes return. These visitations are disorienting, yet strangely consoling. I remember after my cousin Elisabeth died, I dreamed of her, and I said, "But Liz, you are dead!" "I know!" she said, giggling. She seemed quite happy, and who could blame her, as she had been so miserably sick.

—Night likes to send the dead to the dreams of the living. It is one of her favorite tricks.

fact (n.)

1530s, "action, anything done," especially "evil deed," from Latin *factum*, "an event, occurrence, deed, achievement," in Medieval Latin also "state, condition, circumstance," literally "thing done" (source also of Old French *fait*, Spanish *hecho*, Italian *fatto*), noun use of neuter of *factus*, past participle of *facere*, "to do" (from PIE root *dhe-, "to set, put"). Main modern sense of "thing known to be true" is from 1630s, from notion of "something that has actually occurred."

Compare **feat**, which is an earlier adoption of the same word via French. *Facts*, "real state of things (as distinguished from a statement of belief)," is from 1630s. *In fact*, "in reality," is from 1707. *Facts of life*, "harsh realities," is from 1854; euphemistic sense of "human sexual functions" first recorded 1913. Alliterative pairing of *facts and figures* is from 1727.

BEACH

But these

affiliations made further

wounds in the bodies.

Our sentences were vital

but insufficient, our weapons

dull. The landscape gloated,

radiant in an array

of night lights

as the celebrants approached,

their dresses made from wings

of flies and spinning foam,

their shoes from skin

pulled daily from the corpses in sand.

Have a little truth serum to help you

find your way. Born in the

wrong year? Born

of the wrong gender? Born

in the blank house

in which no thing was inflected with

meaning? What is meaning?

The beach the beach the beach.

INVOLUTE

An impermeable layer guards

the sleuth patch, grown

toward rescue, or mission. The quaint,

untranslatable song

forsakes its mild page, unfaithful as ever.

I'm dressed in clouds and they

are smirking at the edge

of late-age homilies, and our poor star

unable to grant its mania to the end of day.

Some patches of seared light, some

plain domestic blues.

There is a stray sense to the air, wind

announcing the eternal

as through an open window, a sister's face.

Things being fetched from afar, from

the imprecision

that gathers any single

into any amount; piles of them, unanchored,

blown every which way.

SUBLIME, FULL

—Evening! A glow of peach and pale blue tonight, signaling the end of summer, with all its accoutrements—tomatoes and grapes and apples and squash—as well as the mutating flora. Good-bye. Now we buckle down into the season that rushes and cools and spills into a rough medley of endings that we watch as they happen, as if the Angel of Transformation had decided to allow her work to be evident and tangible. Day by day, hour by hour, we *witness* change, at once exhilarating and terrifying. Green turns to rust. Rust falls down. This isn't how the sublime came to be, is it?

—Another imponderable, from my point of view, although I must remind you, there have been occasions when what I do was thought to be sublime.

—Hudson River School. And before them, the great J. M. W. Turner, practically the patron saint of sunsets. But I seem to recall that the sublime originally had to do with something distinctly metaphysical, less simply observable. Longinus, right, but what did he say?

—I'm sorry to correct you, but evidently the treatise wasn't by Longinus, but by someone unknown, earlier, in the first century. And I think it was about certain qualities in writing, not nature.

—Thanks. Serves me right, me and my haphazard store of knowledge. But the point is, we don't use the word anymore, except maybe when talking about food. What a *sublime* apple pie! The idea of sublimity has vanished, but why? Where did it go? Now you are almost dark and you have nothing to tell me. Night's Window is about to open. The moon last night was full.

—That's a nice word, *full.*

—Yes, it attaches. I recall a favorite children's book, *Wait Till the Moon Is Full.* But now I wonder if that was its title, or only the refrain of the mother to the little—what were they? raccoons?—wanting to go out but their mother keeps telling them they have to *wait till the moon is full.* The problem with the Internet is that misremembering can be corrected—e.g., Longinus—which is fine, but it means that the odd way we might augment or change or misrecall no longer figures in our capacity to revise or reinvent. All now can be correct. But we need to make mistakes; it's the way of evolution.

sublime (adj.)

1580s, "expressing lofty ideas in an elevated manner," from Middle French *sublime* (15c.), or directly from Latin *sublimis*, "uplifted, high, borne aloft, lofty, exalted, eminent, distinguished," possibly originally "sloping up to the lintel," from *sub-*, "up to" (see **sub-**), + *limen*, "lintel, threshold, sill" (see **limit** (n.)). *The sublime* (n.), "the sublime part of anything, that which is stately or imposing," is from 1670s. For *Sublime Porte*, former title of the Ottoman government, see **Porte**.

full (adj.)

Old English *full*, "containing all that can be received; having eaten or drunk to repletion; filled; perfect, entire, utter," from Proto-Germanic **fulla-*, "full" (source also of Old Saxon *full*, Old Frisian *ful*, Dutch *vol*, Old High German *fol*, German *voll*, Old Norse *fullr*, Gothic *fulls*), from PIE root **pele-* (1), "to fill." Related: *fuller*; *fullest*.

The adverb is Old English *ful*, "very, fully, entirely, completely," and was common in Middle English (*full well, full many*, etc.); sense of "quite, exactly, precisely" is from 1580s. *Full moon*, one with its whole disc illuminated, was Old English *fulles monan*; first record of *full-blood* in reference to racial purity is from 1812. *Full house* is 1710 in the theatrical sense, 1887 in the poker sense (three of a kind and a pair, earlier *full-hand*, 1850). *Full-dress* (adj.), "appropriate to a formal occasion," is from 1761, from the noun phrase.

RELIQUARY

1.

Here in meandered appetite,
our trial by fire becoming
ravenous.

Angel dust. Sense

floats off without comparison
to the Near and the Near's

far example.

Nonsense hitches up her skirt, beckons
the armed boys to follow, singing, she
sings the whole way down the tracks
into the far dry field where hands
of a clock lie pointing. We might have
been lurking or otherwise waiting
but we had forgotten

for what. Thus,

hungers set loose, without a bare
object or thing. As if a statue with a

hole at its center, headless, and
beautiful because we are awed by ruined beauty.

2.

Materialist closet awakens its trove.

An encyclopedia in the ditch

and a child's fervid hand, dallying

under the auspices of dream.

Time for Mistress Nonsense

to resume her spell

and call forth the witch's hat,

the three-cornered Kingdom of Did.

Did not. Did. Ocean in an

envelope of watery air,

child sitting on the beach with a pail.

Descriptive agency

muted against

the arrested cycle. How to

add on, how

turn to that ship

lost in yesterday's fog?

Child buries his arms in sand.

He watches the clouds.

Wind's disobedient push fuels the way.

3.

Hooligan atmosphere of the upswept word,

the traveling Once, partially redeemed

as coupon promise. *Go farther,*

whispers the bad girl from under the tarp.

Go as far as the other side of the moon,

where all the bearers gather to test her gaze.

Cave or tomb, a game of

hounds and jackals. *You go first.*

Picturing the scald of the darkest star.

Picturing the oceanic rule.

Picturing an arrow lodged in an hour

and so tethered to night's

spinning wreath, despite

assemblies of image

high overhead,

folds of winged fire

in the implicate order.

4.

The insufficient cluster

forms its sign. The

instruction, written,

lost among amulets and jewels

of what was once the horizon's tool,

weaving

a prelude, its thought

musical and blind. We might have

resided there, listening

to the thrum and waiting

to catch a glimpse of crimson

on stone, a wound or prayer

where also were found signs of ancestral deeds.

Recursive, in wave patterns, rings of hair and bone.

INTENT, INTEND

—Evening!

I am not unreliable on purpose. I make few promises. My intentions are meant to stick to their resulting actions, but the temporal glue sometimes doesn't hold. I am frequently late, not by much, but by enough to be noticed. And yet I often know the time without looking at a clock. Sometimes I wonder if I simply erase travel time, discount it from my calculations; the mind, anticipating, goes ahead of the body. None of the clocks in my life is exactly correct, which creates a kind of temporal wobble, as if I could make time more indefinite and capacious. But these variations in clock time are not what make me late. I do make promises to myself: *I will do what I say and say what I will do,* and there will be no gaps, no little, jittery tears in the intentional fabric. Yet I seem to have an ability to *unintend,* to keep my intention slightly hidden, even from myself, as if housed in a larger mental space than the narrow one that is volitional, purposeful, directly causal. This suspension is a kind of trust, or perhaps a desire for more than one subject to find its way to its object; a kind of spatial pivot or gyration, complicating the reductive linearity of clock time. Deadlines of all kinds frighten me.

—I can understand that. Could you say more about this pivoting-gyrating idea?

—I can try. I think it's related to art-making. I have said elsewhere that I believe art is how humans have found a way to make objects that serve to introduce each other: one person to another, unknown person. And this motion from known (me, myself) to unknown (you, yourself) is free of fear. I made this. You see, read, hear it. You begin to know something about the "I" that made this, and along with this knowledge perhaps a kind of affinity is awakened, not for the "I" exactly but for the object that the "I" has made. This affinity is a form of desire, an arousal of admiration and curiosity: *how* did she make that? We are baffled, maybe, but we are not fearful. And as we come to know the work, we are changed; our sense of our world is altered.

—OK, I think I follow this. Something about how artworks transfer or translate from person to person.

—Yes, that's about right. A work of art negotiates two subjectivities across spatial-temporal gaps. The first gap occurs in the actual making of the work—in a room, a studio—over however many days, weeks, years. False starts. Revisions. Erasures. Pauses. During this process, time blurs and opens into a manifold, in which the relation of purpose to result is suspended across multiple mental and physical acts: this, not this. Each decision anticipates or conjures the next in an agile, incomplete syntax. The artist loses the *track* of time; time is simultaneously condensed and expanded into the making of the work, and in this duration—Bergson's *la durée*—the artist's intent converts into her interpretation; she forms her way of seeing or knowing her world.

—And the viewer, the reader, obviously is not present for these initial encounters between artist and materials. But the work, when complete, somehow contains them, each minute choice and decision, each change?

—Right. And eventually the thing is made, realized, and makes its way—a second temporal gap—into a more public place—a book, say, or a gallery.

—Travel time. What you don't seem to remember to include in your estimations. From what you are saying, this is a different kind of time than in the actual making of the work, which seems to be within the gyrating and pivoting you were speaking about, where disparate energies collide?

—Well, I'm not sure I would call it a collision; more like simultaneity within a continuum.

—Whoa. You are losing me. I'm getting very cloudy. Can you say something more straightforward about this process?

—OK. We encounter the work of art as the relation that forms between a person, her chosen material, and her world: that is the basic triangle. What is given becomes chosen: that is what *form* is. Form is the witness and result of intention.

intent (n.)

"Purpose," early 13c., from Old French *entent, entente,* "goal, end, aim, purpose; attention, application," and directly from Latin *intentus,* "a stretching out," in Late Latin "intention, purpose," noun use of past participle of *intendere,* "stretch out, lean toward, strain," literally "to stretch out" (see **intend**). In law, "state of mind with respect to intelligent volition" (17c.).

intend (v.)

Circa 1300, *entenden,* "direct one's attention to, pay attention, give heed," from Old French *entendre, intendre,* "to direct one's attention" (in Modern French principally "to hear"), from Latin *intendere,* "turn one's attention, strain (in quest of something), be zealous," literally "stretch out, extend," from *in-,* "toward" (from PIE root **en-,* "in"), + *tendere,* "to stretch," from PIE root **ten-,* "to stretch."

Sense of "have as a plan, have in mind or purpose" (late 14c.) was present in Latin. A Germanic word for this was *ettle,* from Old Norse *ætla,* "to think, conjecture, propose," from Proto-Germanic **ahta,* "consideration, attention" (source also of Old English *eaht,* German *acht*). Related: **intended**; *intending.*

ELISION

These habits within the chamber

of doubt. You

see don't you see

don't you that wild grin

on the face of the madman, you

see the iced rupture

don't you while listening

to a glossy song for

guitar, voice, and piano.

You could swallow these chords.

You could drown in this image.

The hairy trees clustered

stiffly, the bridge in the distance,

the unequivocal train resonating,

the gray bird landing on gray water.

AFTER *AFTER NATURE*

(Note: *After Nature* is a long poem in three parts by W. G. Sebald, written in 1988, translated into English by Michael Hamburger.)

1.

The unsaid strafes its enclosure.

I'm in a store, a storage,

among forgettings that anchor them.

The pasture is all snow and its perceptions

drain the day

outward

onto a disheveled, reckless halo

unspun from a saint's hair

as if scribbled.

The withheld stares

back onto its insolent intention, a girl

in the bridal threshold of a museum,

her white shoulders

readied for sculpture and for the thin fingers

of her groom. Tidy these ancient portals,

says the Bergsonian moon, there's more

to see of the great Rivera murals

whose scansion is blocked

by the banquet's black plumes and

crimson napkins, fake beads of hanging ice.

2.

The baffled children stand their ground.

The boy who cannot smile

the girl who stares into the mutant air

my own mirrored self

dancing in the aisle of beloved

animation, singing along

to a tune rescued and

hidden under soil

piled on the floor in that corner.

That room, that window, those stairs

and across the wide portico a muse

yelling in French

and the mother in pails, the mother in ashes.

And the flowers? you ask. They were

announcements that came slowly up

with the man with a sack on his shoulder.

The snow will not burn but falls as heaving flame.

The drifts are catalytic as they

plummet toward amnesia

and a recessed doll appears, her eyes

painted open.

3.

I did not ask for this bouquet. Please return it.

The form of attention bewilders

and the signal's arc wavers. If I

gaze I gaze, and the blue mountain

is indifferent, like Wittgenstein

staring out from his captive picture.

Some beauties are best left unobserved.

Some dues are best unpaid.

And if Sebald once retrieved

Grünewald's journey,

exposing the throat and often turning

the face towards a blinding light,

then let us be

amazed and wander up a hill

and turn to see

the bereft tribe following Moses

out of Egypt, tracing

the uncertain path into a tent onto which

only a vane fastened with string

remains. The route was written

but the map's insignia and

all the variants of white

dispersed through the holy frame.

4.

Wait here a minute. I need to attend to

the soot. A gashed estrangement

dramatizes the ocular theme.

Rag rag rag. It's a quick refrain,

what a broom might chant.

Accidents happen and rage resumes

under the free rights of dream,

the unsafe conditions

masked by law. The scene

melts into its recursive

harm; the tent

blown up by a young man in the film

of the young man in the film.

The black boy is shot and shot and shot.

Which war are we after? And home

he came smelling of sandalwood and silk,

the scent of beautiful strangers.

The yoked extravagance, the carnal scene,

fire and ice, her crimson

lips stamped on the rim of a glass.

Take them back. The apparition

thwarts declension for the sake of an image.

5.

We settle for stone

even as it attracts disaster

just at the welcoming hour.

Now the exposed branches

have turned yellow, their threads

crawling out from the scripted scene.

Arendt talks about metaphor

enthusiastically; she honors

the sign of what she calls

invisibles,

that which will never attach itself

to thingness. The philosopher's

wonder is fraught; words charge

our love with action

and action blurs syntax. She thinks

we can see what we hear

just as it vanishes.

Chickadees orchestrate

the silence of the hawk's

swerve; all is readied for accounting

as for abstraction.

6.

I liked it better elsewhere,

in the drafty aftermath,

along the dark hall or

sitting on the porch, before the fly

awoke from its winter nap. Up

it crawls on the glacial window.

If I say cardinal, do you see red?

Grace is legible; we collect variously,

accordingly, in the zone

allotted. So a democratic yield

might fashion our taste

for an old sword or a ripe fruit

or the red panoply

of Matisse. Art

moves among us and elicits

the daring collective.

Marvelous and outward we go

toward the plight to heal

what has no mercy, incorporated

as sorrow or bliss, sold separately

to those who come to witness.

7.

Abstraction is invisible; it

pours through the sockets

of the hours and

the broken debris flows

out to sea—a flood of names,

old particulars—

what never was translated;

some drafts on paper—

erode the banks and the banks

rise up into the empty horizon

like nameless cartoon giants.

Be not afraid.

These fives, these tens,

these papered numbers,

watch them change hands

and bring forth shiny gifts.

Dip the oak leaf in gold.

Dip the screen into the rushing waters.

The days will end with or without

portraits. The days will end. *Rag rag.*

to Thomas Wild

CURTAIN (BALTHUS, *LA CHAMBRE*)

Sober dawn
fickle girl
not yet contained
under auspices and
disrobed as by a small god
hidden under fabric
waiting or tethered
to the disbelief that rises
when the next
pleasure, its
particles, smallest of orbs, opens.

FOR NOW

Things that mean so much

little sentiments everywhere

    dust touch

glassy-eyed winter

and so sudden—

    Everything is for now

   hushed

      sled

of twilight

       unbound

from the spool

   unmeasured

        as if indifferent

but for trust's assenting riddle

but for increment—

DESTINY

—Hello, Evening.

—Hi.

—You are shrouded in clouds.

—Yes, we're having a spell of dark weather.

—But at least you know that sooner or later, your radiance will return.

—Yes, but it makes me melancholy, not to be able to have my twilight.

—Well, perhaps I can cheer you up with a quote from the artist William Kentridge.

—You can try.

—It's from his *Six Drawing Lessons*, lectures he gave at Harvard.

—Harvard?

—Never mind. The first lecture is called "In Praise of Shadows."
Listen: *"Let us see where we are. Both receiving all the projections that come toward us, listening, a receiving station, scanning the earth for reports of the world, bombarded by particles of information we cannot escape. And transmitting, projecting, broadcasting ourselves continually. Here I am. HERE I AM. Here I am. And between the two, the receiving station and the transmitting station, all our private engines making sense of the world."* Don't you like that? The idea that "our private engines" are able to make sense of the world?

—I think he exaggerates.

—He *is* oddly optimistic, if that's what you mean by exaggeration, even though he appears to be entirely aware of the dire, incommensurate world we inhabit. If I were he, I would be optimistic, as he seems to revel in a kind of productive chaos; he's like a magician, pulling astonishing images out of, and even as part of, the chancy, shifting plenitude of things. I sometimes think he is more a force of nature than merely human.

—There are such humans. Ovid, for example.

—Ovid?

—Yes, his recitation of transformations between the realm of the gods and the realm of the human, all of it somehow mediated by or through nature.

—That's true.

—You sound like Glaucon answering Socrates. Not so much answering as agreeing.

—That's backward: from Ovid's Rome to Plato's Greece.

—I don't worry about these calendar constraints. It's all the same for me what you earth persons do with your days and years and when you do them.

—Does that mean you have no sense of chronology?

—Well, I must, since that *chrono-* in *chronology* refers to time, on which I am entirely dependent, but I don't have any need or use for calendars or for clock time, which are how humans convert life into numbers.

—Well, not just numbers: they are how we come to know about sequences, individual and historical; how we measure cause and effect: *con/sequences*: with sequences. It's the way we find order, even as we think in terms of generations, and seem to lock persons into their age groups. Everyone wants to know the year of your birth. Why? As if it were the most important, defining aspect of your being.

—Ah, yes, the measurements are often inaccurate, propelled by the collecting data machines, the algorithms, deleting oddness and variation and turning your life into received ideas, data *about* your life. And then you—they—call attention to the exception. Is this how celebrity happens, the cultivation of the exception?

—Good question. Celebrity seems to shift normal into abnormal, persons into things or objects, and in this shift, other consequences occur.

—Such as?

—Well, you know, once you are in the realm of celebrity, you begin to behave like Ovid's gods, willfully indifferent to ordinary behaviors and their accepted moral and ethical constraints. Our world is beset by these figures at the moment.

—Ah, power. Another condition I am so happy not to know, except by the engines that soar across me on their way elsewhere, carrying bunches of you humans to their chosen destinations. *Jerusalem, Athens, Alexandria, Vienna, Bangkok, Aleppo.*

—We cannot choose our destiny.

—No, but you can say *here I am.*

destiny (n.)

> Mid-14c., from Old French *destinée* (12c.), "purpose, intent, fate, destiny; that which is destined," noun use of fem. past participle of *destiner*, from Latin *destinare*, "make firm, establish" (see **destination**). The sense is of "that which has been firmly established," as by fate.

CATBIRD

1.

Profuse song: secular, unrequited,
a motion toward and away, repeated.

The stamp is hopping but nothing
has been sent. Conditions are green

but the mind foils the season
in atrocities, intimate, obscene.

Let's cross the dream bridge.
Why not invite those who appear

numbered under the guise of
care, the few not yet drowned.

The greens are already tired
in the roar of hot motors

heaving upstream under
the weight of darker mountains.

Bird says *la petite la petite*
grieving, or adjusting, its nonsense.

2.

Hot night goes rogue onto pink horizon.
Flesh in the sky, et cetera. Our own

arrested development, the ones
next door thwarted.

Elsewhere is here! Voice
traces the abnegation of souls

that change only as addiction.
OK, go to Greece. Go to your island.

Leave us in the fumes of evening,
the minor scars of omission.

Dark mountain wearing its gown.
Peonies open to violation.

3.

A silence blooms in rehearsal.
Shade targets an unmolested patch

reverting to horizontal, landscape-style.
There's plenty of documentary evidence

to film if you can get the killers
to speak. Later, a prize. Later, an offering

as apology to the millions slain.
Catbird says *I believe I believe*

cresting the hemlock, clad in gray robes.
It has been to the temple

but the flies are hungry; always in
mourning, they crave salty hair.

Something to dig, something to mend.
The quilts of Gee's Bend, Alabama,

redolent in recollection, abstracted
from all weathers, heat, cold, heat.

In whose army? Blistering obedience
under the chill moon; following after.

Look! Do not find. Look again!
Do not find. Heart's repetitions stitched on.

4.

Interlopers stride along in search
of Poussin's snake in the long twilight,

or dawn. They find an inner tube
at the side of a lake, oily and deflated.

The crest of desire; a
terrified tourist stooping for shells

along the coast. Bird says, *Give it up!*
Give it up! go back to the cottage garden,

the yellowy smear of pollinated
dust where unnatural acts pillage

the very silence Poussin was eyeing.
Your nails are a mess. The ground

needs sweeping. Forget the
improvised setting of the singing

bird's makeshift melody:
her sequence will not end.

But her broken nest annuls
transparency, and the withered branch.

The noisy men persist, gunning
their engines up the small hill.

Above, a silver cloud, rain tarnished,
and the hectic sound of the fearless young.

WARNING (OVID)

Windy hair

kiss the ocean spray

watch out for the   winged thing watch out for the tree

its branching arms   embrace   unto

And the mouth

                      spills out and the owl

has night in its eyes

and the girl

has spread her legs into a spider's web

caught in the branches of the changed tree

watch out for the peak

daylight drags its morphological shift

into view

   while there is no moon

only the allegory of desire

watch out for the wordy violation

ordinance of song   the viola and the rapid lapse

perhaps those five stars are a   constellated bear

      or goblet of ink

            origin smashed among the rocks

                  little boat tossed

metamoments argue the toss   cartoon flares

doubt by trickery   sleight of hand sight gag   over she goes

and comes out a statue a god a flower

girl found on the banks

the peacock saw it   eyes flair into feathered arcs

logo pasted on stone

rubbed off

as the argument

takes and then

falters without a proper

condition

to become another

bird after bird identical shapes

tossed skyward

light splintered

        into molecular arcs

bewitched by rain

man into stone   stone into the river's

        refusal of time.

JURY

Stale bondage: history's messed-up parade

of the undone. Nor dare

locute after the fact's act, nor say, having told. Old

unmerciful conditions speeding inkjet

gloss rammed down the starving throats of

children. *Children*: a sign, not pointing, *children*.

Blast of bright color from nature's pile.

As if evidence could return to be newly

considered, appraisals gathered for a final auction

under the golden tent. Stale bondage. Mistrial.

SPELL

We know, again from the experts, that Jovellanos, when Goya painted his portrait, had just been appointed the king's "minister of grace and justice." This was as much of a liberal, Enlightenment moment—a few months in late 1797 and early 1798—as Spain ever had.

—T. J. Clark

1.

So, then, where is our

Minister of Grace and Justice,

our minister

for the end of ignorance under the law?

The law's vulgate. *Zap, zap,*

you're dead. Zap for good measure.

Goya's interior spreads

cartoon stain, red

into the black garb of sabotage.

                 And there, in that city, light

shatters into

debris—glass, coin,

shoe, book. Book?

Look! Look! Can you see the book?

The pages are wet. Can you turn them?

Place your thumb in oil. Blot the spiral out.

2.

History's horizon

blurs into running crowds,

pitched waves, mobile boundaries

not sanctioned by law. History's

horizon

contracts into small boats

traversing rough waters.

Scan the sky's evening,

golds and greens

more brilliant than a reliquary chalice,

a saint's crescent. *Paint that.* Scan

the turbulence for cinders,

white-hot dots.   Matrix

       of illusion, spurred on by desire and

            reason's catastrophic carrier

                pregnant with a god. Sappho's moon

             crossed by the wing of an owl. Dear gray-eyed

           Athena, please allow

transport

safely across the waters. *Film that.*

3.

Trapped by a ghost, many ghosts, a host

of ghosts. They

do not sing

but stare into a shade

lowered over coins

that mimic sun.

The young man

on the screen is timeless.

He speaks into the unknown

from a blackened room. We cannot

see his interlocutors nor hear their exhaled

breath. Meanwhile, in the stadium, thousands

stand to sing in unison

an anthem.

> *O say can you see by the dawn's*

remnant

bombs bursting air. *Record that.*

4.

The agenda has a requiem—

brass, percussion, solo baritone

rising over the choral bloom.

Look up and up, the cascade rises!

But the leaves are fallen

and the familial roost divided:

the plural of I *is not* we.

       And in the not we, we

             flee

      into the hedge while the machines

   routine their killer noise.

Let's improvise a story. Let's begin

with a journey out

onto paths, into meadows, glades,

forests, brackish ponds, scented

lilies on ponds, bees.

Let's end with a prayer for the bees.

5.

Or these words: *cyber, black,*

blessings to spell forth

gifts. Good luck with that and with picking

shards from the pavement oil.

Pilgrim or migrant or

exile traversing the calendar's stage

with spidery precision. Speak

into the megaphone: *cyber, black.*

Now join the ensemble as it

wanders from what it was taught

by a preacher, a cop, saved

from the whispering echo:

I want, I want.

6.

How to quantify a rupture? Sit in its midst

like a bad child in mud. Discipline

and punish. Good luck with that.

The global ruse is insupportable

by the local client; she

wants the garden stone

lowered so her child can reach

parsley, sage, rosemary,

and thyme, lyrics

from the melting pot. Let's poll the pot

and see how it intends to vote.

Zap. Let's take a bite from the apple.

Whim over the doorframe, tears in the sink.

7.

Lady natters on about intimacy. She's a bore

but she's cornered the market

on intimacy.

She tells us we

need to speak face-to-face, into

the ensemble of relations that faces are. She

warns against the mirror at our fingertips.

Are you tired of these homilies, these

warnings, these studies that say

we have lost touch? We

know we have lost touch. We

know we are the remnant organs of a bodiless hum.

8.

So an unnamed subject bequeaths

golds, greens, all its auras

into our show. Don't look now.

Turn away as the hero

walks across a bridge with his

murderer mistress. He walks

with a side-to-side motion, his great shoulders

tipping. The water below carries his coat

on sorrow's bloodied current.

It's an affecting image of the unendurable

endurance of duration, phenomenal

and cruel. The thing disintegrates, or melts,

like paper in a flood, becoming illegible

as it falls over the embankment.

The hero Luther is named for the hero Luther.

9.

Pick a card, any card.

What did you get? A nine? A queen?

Which? One with black spades or

one with red hearts? Place your bets.

Let's get a slice of pizza.

Let's pick up some eggs, some chard.

Let's go down to the river

and watch the sun set.

Let's hope for the best.

                          The clock is imaginative; it

has time or we imagine it has time.

I'm not sure how to measure

this gift, sanctioned by the stars. They

stay constant although they are dead.

They send what came before what

came last: their light, aftermath.

CHEER

—Hello.

—Did you sleep well?

—I don't sleep. I vanish forever. Did you?

—Not particularly. I have holes in my sleep.

—Holes?

—Yes, I awaken in the small hours of the morning and I can't get back to sleep. It's as if an Ambassador has been sent from the Undone World, which must be part of Night's Empire, to read a list of the things I am supposed to do, to have already done. I have no way to get rid of this figure and the minutes turn into hours until finally I take a pill and then sleep but I wake up feeling already depleted, and so the morning begins badly. I would like to wake up cheerful and animated, ready to embark on these tasks.

—You have a puritanical streak.

—Yes. There are Puritans in my family history. They did not approve of enthusiasm. There was a portrait I recall of a thin-lipped, joyless, censorious couple. They stared down at us in my aunt and uncle's living room. I seem to have inherited some of these traits, but they are in direct contradiction to my pleasure-seeking self, which, I admit, mostly dominates.

—Except in the small hours when Night's Ambassador of the List is in charge.

—You are reminding me of a passage in Nietzsche, from his preface to *On the Genealogy of Morals*. As you know, he undertakes to figure out origins of the ideas of good and evil and so discover their actual value or meaning. He talks about the English, in particular a certain Dr. Rée. Sorry, Evening, I have to interrupt this. The noon whistle just went, and as it did I looked up and saw a bluebird.

—And so?

—Bluebirds make me think that there is magic in the world.

—Magic?

—Yes, magic as a form of unexpected cheer; bluebirds definitely cheer me. So, then, as I was about to quote, from Nietzsche: *"For cheerfulness— or in my own language gay science—is a reward: the reward of a long, brave, industrious, and subterranean seriousness, of which, to be sure, not everyone is capable. But on the day we can say with all our hearts, 'Onwards! Our old morality too is part of the comedy!' we shall have discovered a new complication and possibility for the Dionysian drama of 'The Destiny of the Soul'—and one can wager that the grand old eternal comic poet of our existence will be quick to make use of it!"* He had such a wild mind, don't you think? So many different impulses found in his verbal lexicon, so you are always off-balance, and you can't quite tell when he is being serious and when he is teasing your own seriousness by ironic mockery. If I recall, Nietzsche's first subject was philology. He seems to have loved language.

cheer (n.)

Circa 1200, "the face, countenance," especially as expressing emotion, from Anglo-French *chere*, "the face," Old French *chiere*, "face, countenance, look, expression," from Late Latin *cara*, "face" (source also of Spanish *cara*), possibly from Greek *kara*, "head," from PIE root **ker-** (1), "horn; head." From mid-13c. as "frame of mind, state of feeling, spirit; mood, humor."

By late 14c. the meaning had extended metaphorically to "state or temper of mind as indicated by expression." This could be in a good or bad sense ("The feend . . . beguiled her with treacherye, and brought her into a dreerye cheere," "Merline," c. 1500), but a positive sense, "state of gladness or joy" (probably short for *good cheer*), has predominated since c. 1400.

Meaning "that which makes cheerful or promotes good spirits" is from late 14c. Meaning "shout of encouragement" is first recorded 1720, perhaps nautical slang (compare earlier verbal sense, "to encourage by words or deeds," early 15c.). The antique English greeting *what cheer?* (mid-15c.) was picked up by Algonquian Indians of southern New England from the Puritans and spread in Indian languages as far as Canada.

—*to Marina van Zuylen*

KITH

What's the dollar, love? We be
dissembling under the stars, the stores, and
herein birth's mighty smile, simplest of apertures.
Into which: a spate of verbs, or swallowing,
the wing and throat,
the bird and a damp tunnel of shift,
appetite and simple forgetting
as you notice the moment when
what might have occurred went blank.
Some Latin phrase here would be useful.
Some sign of tears wet enough to wipe
up after you, specific and not, you and not,
stayed by our restless sorrow, our mute flight.

IDES

Then,
when no longer part of the scheme
dream of giving
living in the lap of stuff
rough inheritance from one to the other
mother to daughter, daughter to ought
caught without requisite offspring
spring makes her uneasy
queasy in the robes
globe's spin, increased light
ignites desire among the skin's
dins of hatching
attaching this one to that
cat to prey, mud
flood anointing the shabby woods
goods for nesting robins and their mates
fates in the blues
of a saint's dress, Mary's news
received as quantum
leap without origin or sum.

EROS

—Good morning, Evening.

—Hi.

—I'm in a poor state of mind. There's an incessant turbulence in my soul about which I seem able to do nothing. Some collision of near and far, as if I were living on a hair or seam, thinly precarious, unable to withstand a mere breeze. There is no breeze; the trees, their branches, are as still as road signs. I am feeling mentally fatigued and a desire to settle into something that has no reason to be, some pre-articulate, ruminating stare. And to make matters worse, in my inner ear, song lyrics, repeating and repeating so that I begin to think my brain is heading off into a *never-never land* of banal sentimentality without my mind's permission. The tune and its lyrics are just there, carrying on all day and into the night unless I do something to stop them.

—What might that be?

—I'm not sure. Maybe only something intensely physical would work.

—Such as?

—I don't know. Swimming. Dancing. Sex.

—I am not familiar with sex, as I don't copulate; I simply subside. What about it?

—Well, I'm not sure I can tell you about it, as it seems to have vanished from my life, except in dreams. The apparent consensus is that desire diminishes for women as we age, despite the protestations of Jane Fonda and Erica Jong. *To desire, to be desired.* It seems to come down to bodies in some mechanistic, cosmetic way. Why are you smiling?

—Because all I do is change and people seem to love it.

—They love to watch change, but they don't want it to happen to them. And your changing isn't the same as aging.

—What about sex?

—For me, it was consuming and animating and extravagant, if I can say something so odd. I confused it, desire, my own as well as when it came toward me, so many times with love, or the possibilities for love. Love as a kind of pop song.

—I am glad to say I have no idea what these words refer to. Do you want to tell me more?

—No, I don't want to extend these tepid, revelatory remarks; they are in danger of turning into confession, and yet I suppose *sex* is only a trope for the conditions of intimacy, intimate knowledge. Something about physical contact gives us an entirely different sense of each other. It's another kind of language, and without it, we are left in the realm of the mind and the mind's coordinates, perception without touch.

—Intimate knowledge of something isn't the same as knowledge of intimacy with someone, if I follow you.

—You follow me, yes, but you see, we can go only so far together along this word path. In fact, maybe it isn't sex, the act, I'm really talking about, but Eros itself, the basic animating engine of discovery that belongs to all living creatures and, in humans, fuels aspiration as well as curiosity. I think this is what William Blake believed.

—Blake! His angels fly by from now to now, singing in unison.

—And I was just reading what Yeats had to say about Blake's idea of the imagination. Listen to this:

> *Imagination divides us from mortality by the immortality of beauty, and binds us to each other by opening the secret doors of all hearts. He cried again and again that every thing that lives is holy, and that nothing is unholy except things that do not live—lethargies, and cruelties, and timidities, and that denial of imagination which is that root they grew from in old times. Passions, because most living, are most holy—and this was a scandalous paradox in his time— and man shall enter eternity borne upon their wings.*

That's from *Ideas of Good and Evil.* My copy belonged to my grandmother. She signed it: *Elisabeth Lloyd 1910.* I wonder if she read it.

—Have the lyrics to the song abated?

—Gone.

Eros (n.)

God of love, late 14c., from Greek *eros* (plural *erotes*), "god or personification of love"; literally "love," from *eran*, "to love," *erasthai*, "to love, desire," which is of uncertain origin.

Freudian sense of "urge to self-preservation and sexual pleasure" is from 1922. Ancient Greek distinguished four ways of love: *erao*, "to be in love with, to desire passionately or sexually"; *phileo*, "have affection for"; *agapao*, "have regard for, be contented with"; and *stergo*, used especially of the love of parents and children or a ruler and his subjects.

PALM

You keep turning up in my dreams

like a penny, worth less than the old,

but shinier. I am glad to hold you

in my warm hand and

turn you face up, stare into your

eyes looking at me. Hello, I say,

and you say it back to me, like the gypsy

in the song

who disappears at the end.

I vow never to spend you

even in this

unrequited bliss field

with all the shades drawn down.

KISS

Yes, *the trees seem to agree*, but
I'm caught in the near
distance, wound into small parcels.
Your tongue. My
mouth. The dust
off the rugs, too, swept
onto a vehicle, with a bug
for good luck. Did you look up,
or away? And as for the birds, you
have elicited their cry
from far, far off, like the whistle
of a train, the hum of its engine
going someplace else.

MONODY

And here we are in the hour of the spider,

time slows in variant transfer,

sadder than moon and the inconsequential

netting of another dead insect

in the turn's turn,

accidental rhythms and sticky notes

up on a surface and there dwelling at peace

once thought unimaginable on the quick road.

Slows for sorrow

to reflect how it went

speeding toward the final episode when

the first and second had been omitted,

the third misrecalled. We were

enchanted, climbing the hill in search

of honey or waiting at the curb

for the light to change

or falling onto the deepest stake

driven into the enflamed

white passages between high branches.

VERDI

Ego on the salty shoals, distributed as ghost.

Ghost being no thing, no instance, no bug.

Maximum and minimum exercise their skills

saying more or less the same thing differently.

What tells the telling? You fathomed and

your stride collapsed the little targets

along the way: lamppost, bed, drum.

Now the assembly has left the stage,

this time in a hurry for the exits, lest

the alarm sound and they are made to stay

fastened to their roles: Otello, or Louisa.

May I have this dance? Don't mind my cast,

it comes off at night and turns into a wand

to wave the lovers back into their first embrace.

PARADIGM

—Evening!

—Hello.

—The light is exceptionally fine.

—Yes. Thank you. It is my own. I'm an expert at fine lighting.

—There's an elaborate, finely spun spiderweb in the corner of the window. The light, your light, is illuminating it; radiant colors slide along the filaments when I move my head.

—Those are not mine. They belong to Night's Window: not sufficiently scenic, too minutely quixotic. I'm involved in spatial vistas: clouds and shadows cast by trees across meadows and, of course, my famous sunsets.

—The actual scene out the window is still just now, seemingly not mutable, an illusion caused by no wind, as in a painting. What do you mean, *Night's Window?*

—When you open Night's Window, things from *before* or *after* flow in, in no particular order or sequence. It's the space of the temporally incommensurate.

—Dreams.

—Yes, dreams and all the other collisions and collusions of memory and anticipation.

—That could be useful, I guess, if unsettling. Speaking of which, I've just been reading the French philosopher Jacques Rancière.

—I'm not sure I know him. Possibly he is a morning writer.

—I want to be a morning writer, but I fear I am an evening writer. Or maybe both, but they are different. I have a sense that a morning writer is more acute and clear than an evening writer.

—Why?

—Coffee as opposed to wine. Wine makes you imagine that things are more luminous than they are.

—I don't imagine anything other than things as they are.

—I didn't mean you; I meant me.

—Pronouns. I am glad not to have to bother with them. What about this Jacques Rancière?

—He thinks against accepted opinions about important issues, although really I hate that word.

—Which word?

—*Issues*. Not the word, obviously, but what it suggests about how we engage our mutual worlds, by taking up, dealing with *issues*. Usually through complaint and grievance; usually, from the point of view of the person or persons who feel aggrieved, so there is nearly always a suggestion that someone is wrong and someone has been wronged and that there is a definite right. I think the way to change things as they are is by behaving differently, and that means thinking differently, shifting perceptions, imagining yourself in another's place. I often tell students to imagine they did not write what they wrote, and read it as if they were someone else. It's a thought experiment.

—And Rancière?

—I want to say he wants to *awaken* us to possibilities.

—Maybe he *is* a morning writer; the dream space is useful for awakening possibilities, especially if you are able to stay close to air that comes through the Night's Window.

—Are you jealous of Morning?

—Yes, somewhat. What possibilities does this Rancière wish to awaken?

—I think he wants to suggest or possibly create links between politics and aesthetics, to insert or assert our capacity to imagine and create into our sense of a politics. I suppose ultimately he wants us to bring these two worlds, these potentials, into a single frame, but not by addressing *issues*. I am thinking about these things, Evening, because even the young artists I know are beginning to think like bean counters and rationalists, the numbers gang, who imagine, for example, that sexism and racism can be mitigated by keeping count.

—You have a thing about numbers. Quantifying.

—Yes, I think these realities can be addressed only by immersion in an entwined animation of knowledge with imagination. You know, putting what is the case against what could be the case, where the second case is not based on practical expedience and numerological projection but on something more risky.

—Risky how?

—Because not yet known.

—Like weather, not always predictable.

—Maybe. More like what happens to the sky when the sun goes down.

—Thank you. I take that as a compliment. You think the great problems of the age can be solved by being more like sunsets.

—Well, no. I'm trying to talk about art-making as a paradigm.

—That's quite fancy.

—I wish I had a fresher vocabulary.

—I do, too, and it's getting late. I'm about to retire.

—OK, I understand. Perhaps we need to open the window and let Night in.

—Be careful. Night comes in many guises, not all of them good. She takes up with some scary characters as she travels around the globe; she has the entire universe from which to draw, and all its history.

—Nightmares.

—Yes, those dark horses she likes to ride. But she also likes to summon.

—Summon?

—Yes, to peer into the forgotten and the secret and drag forth their untethered souls and remnant loose ends, and insert them into the sleeping mind. You think that your dreams are yours only, but they are not; they are connected up to all the other sleepers.

—Walt Whitman.

—Yes, that famous passage in *Leaves of Grass* where everyone is sleeping and, in sleep, all are equal to each other. Whitman saw how Night works. He had a tendency toward universalism that allowed him to draw on particulars.

—I don't quite follow you.

—Well, I'm fading, so I can't be more lucid. But I saw an essay recently that talks about Whitman as paradigm.

—I like that word, *paradigm.*

paradigm (n.)

Late 15c., from Late Latin *paradigma*, "pattern, example," especially in grammar, from Greek *paradeigma*, "pattern, model; precedent, example," from *paradeiknynai*, "exhibit, represent," literally "show side by side," from *para-*, "beside" (see **para-** (1)), + *deiknynai*, "to show" (cognate with Latin *dicere*, "to show"; from PIE root ***deik-**, "to show," also "pronounce solemnly"). Related: *paradigmatic*; *paradigmatical*.

PARTITA

I might have done a better job of hearing
the song, its lyrics, so difficult now, but
then, because we sang along, and the melody
sweet, everyone agreed, in unison, and there
wasn't a tax bill in sight.
Where were you? the children ask.
Under the canopy, I said,
under the tent. Under the tune of days
when we joined as a matter of course
and were not accosted by lost words.
And now? they ask. And now, I said, I listen.

HYMN

Go down: striven darken under

trim vestibule, autopilot *zaum*

trashed excelsior, dread canoe, travel exec

martyred, deer-eyed, flat-coated—

go down! Vanished, boulevard,

some numerology, some spin

word-crossed, sponged, the bloods of those

passing. Passing in the hurtled rigor

over which the unhurt star shines blankly.

Now heat. Now lavish dreams, critical

embargoes against *all who enter here*.

Sentences contract, mouth dry, eyes

watching eye dust assemble

a canopy of killers

and their toys. More heat. More

screams in a tide, blurry workers

leaving the factory forever. Unhurt

but for dozens flailing on the pavement.

References elude, shape of fear, phrase

by phrase; a doctor-priest

present in the confidential room

initialing scripts. Illegal sound

so loud you can hear a bomb drop.

Boiled down, icon, essence.

In the dust, the final phase, jokes

to the howling, fire-spitting wind.

Cocktails served at the darkened embassy.

Say something real. Say Barcelona,

Paris, Madrid. Say London.

Say the vehicle is a white van.

Brooklyn. Not essence, the name

of the real not an essence.

Rapture of the kill's

postliterary strophe, transcendent

delirium, crescendo

no one sees before the film's

transcription: single hurt color, luminous spiral.

World bloom. Cartwheel. What acid

punctuation filters drawn pistols,

scar wounds his perfect face, drawn

across like a river on a map.

Boundaries test aptitude for strangers.

Such love arose in the early hours, among

a generation's lurid games,

disobedience charmed by facile profits.

And now? Now crouches, muddied by then.

Go back! Evidence, hidden

under the story's pleasure chest

and the garden in sudden eclipse

so dark we could not find

the merely real, leaf, color, paper

trail logged out and the remainder

cramped in the compost. What name

to give? Trial and error,

trial by error, watching as the ship goes down.

Go down, Moses. Choir

sings to the scrap of mountain

visible over the looming willow.

I'm in the seventh chamber

of the vicarious hotel, under spread

sheets where resemblance begets

resemblance in a rectangular, acrid

light. I am, as usual, counting my sins.

Tell old Pharaoh to let my people go.

WILDERNESS

—Evening! I am now remembering, again, how, after my father died, I was conscious of the things in the house that he had touched, that had touched him, and how these things took on an almost sacred aura, as if by touching them I was still in touch with him. So, even now, his massive, worn *Webster's* dictionary sits in the front hall, and his single clear paperweight that fits in the palm of your hand is on my desk.
—Absence embodied as presence. A kind of paradox.
—They inflect my world, these objects whose meanings are found not in their intrinsic value but in their affective surround, so to speak: their associations with persons and places, and the actual physical realities evoked by them.
—Memory's crowded lanes.
—Not quite memories but something even more vaguely elusive, maybe not even sayable. Does everyone have these trinkets, endowed with particulars of private, subjective meaning? I often make habitats for them, topological vignettes or scenes in which they sit like figures in a child's phantasm. A tiny, bent metal cow or sheep bell bought in a market outside of Barcelona with the English artist Richard Hamilton; my mother's single turquoise earring, part of a pair given to her by one of her lovers; a tiny dish with a creature painted on it bought from a Hopi child in Second Mesa, Arizona, when I was seventeen and visiting my boyfriend Fred, whose mother lived in Santa Fe. There are many of these objects, meaningless to others. The entire mantelpiece is a narrative made of them: postcards, figurines, rocks, dice, the dragon from Nepal my godfather, Tom, gave me when I graduated from college, saying, "This will bring magic into your life." Sentiment, for sure, but also triggers of connection; they produce sensuous mindscapes, completely different from photographs, as they refer to the tactile or haptic surround that allows memory to feel active and embodied. Without these associations these objects are truly worthless, and I sometimes imagine them being tossed into the trash after I die, to

the irritation of whoever will have to deal with the detritus of my life: a motley, ephemeral inheritance.

—That's a bit mawkish.

—Yes, I guess. Still, the curious thing is, I arrange them into new topoi; I release them from their original place and time and then see how they perform with strangers, so to speak. I suppose it's a kind of visual, material syntax.

—They are all your own private objective correlatives, incomplete transitional objects, metonymies or substitutions, which you can care for and control, unlike living persons. They stand in for those you love.

—That's a sobering thought.

—Well, now that you say it, I think it is about sobriety of a kind, a way to intervene on your mother's drunkenness and the chaos it caused in the household of your young self. You spent so much time wishing for your world to be lucid, ordered, and fresh, when it was so often incoherent and fetid.

—This is true. In fact I came to think of my mother as a wilderness, simultaneously beautiful and frightening, and even now, so long after she perished, my world is always partly on the verge of collapse and ruin, a disorder that wants or waits to be ordered. It's a perverse way of holding on to her, I suppose.

—Yes, I have observed this. It happens to your garden.

—It is a rhythm of alternating dissonance and consonance, and I think my poems are like that as well, veering toward frictions or fragments that resist rules of syntax.

—You aren't very good with rules. You don't take instruction well.

—True.

wilderness (n.)

> Circa 1200, "wild, uninhabited, or uncultivated place," with **-ness** + Old English *wild-deor*, "wild animal, wild deer"; see **wild** (adj.) + **deer** (n.). Similar formation in Dutch *wildernis*, German *Wildernis*, though the usual form there is *Wildnis*.

NAVE

Or such incentives as a golden
hook dangling from the neck
of a swan. Glint of moon.
Circumference
of a pond and the
incessant vibration of wings.
A song off in the distance,
song, or chant. Above
a yellow willow
the feminine
drift of clouds,
gauzy and unpredictable,
secrets intact. And
the devotional
sun ruptures its coil
and leaks through,
long fingers
of tarnished light
touching a bowl.
Pews, aisles, heads
bowed to stone. Above
the willow, clouds
assemble a congregation
of weeping girls,
their heads wrapped
in bandages, feet
muddied. None of this
can be seen.
So the dream
sutures images

onto pale drawings:
here will be the bed,
here the gown; here
will be the drain
for the new sink, here
the table, candle, spoon.
And these? Stairs,
folded out from air
and stars, made
to lean against a broken
stump. Up, up, down, down,
counting the steps
as the river disappears
behind a looming scaffold.
This would have a name
but it is mute as weather
and the thin poles
are transparent
to the sound of bells
heaving their toll.
Havoc? Is this havoc?
The dogs are loosed.
In the dream, we
climbed like children,
counting *one, two, three*
up the ancient
ladder with its scent of pine.
A man played a cello.
A woman lay
prone on a deck,
turning into the stench
of salt and tobacco, her
hair flooding

across the hull. I guess
a band played
to keep the ritual intact
but the sea
and the sails
and the moving clouds
heard nothing of the repeated
drum pulse. The woman drowned.
Molecular and luminous
she assembled in front of a cave
where hands had touched rock
and rock became bird.

The anchor's chain rains down
link by link, in a clatter of
hardened soot.
Have we been here before?
The interior doubles its enclosure;
a circus forms. A mountain
is a bruise on the horizon
but the sky, hidden again,
continues to harbor
the girls' undistributed lament.
Pale light; virtue in long
rags pulls across
a blind little passage.
Were we ever inside?
And yet the glass
broke into glittery shards
and the freed bloods
crossed the floor, the gravel,
the fields. And water?
Yes, water

fell for the architect
and for the carnival jester
and for the improbable swan.
Memory's fraudulent
desire strips
rapture onto fable.
Soldier standing in front
of a statue. Woman
in floral robe.
Bricks of the missing house.
Turn down that street
sit on that porch
watch those roof cats
scatter for their prey.
Is murky now, and the dark
contracts its allegory
into testaments of faith.
We are waiting
for a crumpled assonance
to undo the cries
for mercy, or make
from artifice an actual tool.
The dump contracts our purview.
We count blue bottles
thrown from the sea,
toss gray pebbles
at empty jars. Choice
is consequence.
Were we
wearing hoods that day?
Which day? The day
the clown
climbed all the way

to the top and stared down.
Neither extended nor reached.
Habit's insatiable laps,
roving in orbits,
their bright slogans
drawn into icons of intent.
What shall we do? What do?
The bridge hangs over
the river, a diadem of light.
And the silent drone
traverses the amphitheater
from above, unblinking
dry eye on the rubble lot.
The clown scowls
through his mute mask, unable
to know how many, how
much. He spins
a toy top, he
pinches the air.
There are constellations
sieving the night,
equations
distorting the aperture
—this does not
equal this. Into the aporia
floats the sum of disbelief
as the parable
calls up its miraculous
lyric—*was blind but now*—

to Dan Beachy-Quick

CAPTURE (LUCRETIUS)

World consists
of an infinite

particles of
knowledge and beauty

things that follow
no orthodoxy

punishments

rewards
as durable

fragile

including
to disappear

anyway

second place
the winner

except

for Rome
humanists

culture

somewhere
library

slipped

to search
obscure

accidents
swerve

dust

for something
to find anything

at that moment

and copied.

SCRAP

Other than what is

        without saying

      or motion
  still

crouched below
our intensity   made blank

not to be captured

     by delay or

any last resort

      the hollow stump's

armless chair

    ricochet passages

to desire   to endow   to hold.

SOLSTICE

The unknown brackets its invaluable task.
This was a parade but now

the pale sky is pouring itself
into the river

and the phantom toy whale
smiles with silver teeth at raw,

meticulous wrappings
in the season of fragments.

Joy constructs its message, a
moon, or doll, and

the windows, all of them, fabricated
in China where I thought you

had been. Have you been to China?
You, there, in the window,

where a boat and a ball
dwell under the eyes of an angel.

It's an enjambment and a plenum,
twilight's ribbony flow,

furnace purring, the lamps
tidy under their circumferences

cast down with the dissolution
of ambient decor, spreading

clouds of semblance,
the crowd coming to the rescue

brave with glassy retrieval,
miracle dark, briefest illumination.

for David Levi Strauss and Sterrett Smith

PHENOMENON

—Why does it take so long for knowledge to inform behavior?

—Not my kind of question, as I am blissfully free of both concepts.

—Don't prevaricate. Just because you don't do something doesn't mean you can't understand it. This is the premise of psychology, just for starters, not to mention the entire premise of a liberal arts curriculum.

—You are the one who believes in doing as a way to knowing, not I. It's your infatuation with the thinking of John Dewey.

—OK. Maybe my quandary can be traced back to Dewey's ideas of learning by doing, and his comforting notion that *an* experience is, or can be, aesthetic; that the aesthetic engages our entire being. Perhaps, I am thinking now, aesthetic experiences are the agent of the integration of our beings into not so much coherent, singular selves as sites of immersive attention and response that allow us to change. Dewey wrote, "An object is peculiarly and dominantly esthetic, yielding the enjoyment characteristic of esthetic perception, when the factors that determine anything which can be called *an* experience are lifted high above the threshold of perception and are made manifest for their own sake."

—That sounds good, but I am not sure I understand it.

—I know, it's not entirely clear what these "factors" are that become manifest for their own sake, but still, there is something here that allows for any experience, any object, to be lifted "above the threshold of perception." I think he is speaking about things that stay in one's awareness after their occurrence, and shift our store of knowledge. Knowledge, he says somewhere, is always in the past. His emphasis on the present seems a specifically American way of understanding both the experimental method and history, our sometimes heedless rush away from what was, into the unknown, which we confuse, often, with the new. Now we are faced with a present that seems stripped of embodied presence, much less knowledge of the past. We seem to be living in a steady stream of *nows*. Dewey wrote, "Art celebrates with peculiar intensity the moments in which the past reinforces the present and in which the future is a quickening of what now is."

—Well, I don't know. I am present but I have neither past nor future; and I don't stay.

—Does that make you a fiction? You aren't a work of art.

—Well, maybe not, but I seem to elicit them regularly. I exist, but not exactly as a thing.

—But I perceive you.

—Yes, you perceive me, but you don't actually get to have or capture me; I don't seem to fit into Dewey's idea of the aesthetic, but you and everyone else swoon when I am particularly pretty.

—I do take many photos of you.

—*I have no this; I have only is.* I am everywhere and you are somewhere, and I am always changing. I am not a thing.

—Ah, a phenomenon.

—That's a nice word. It seems to fit me to a T.

phenomenon (n.)

> 1570s, "fact, occurrence," from Late Latin *phœnomenon*, from Greek *phainomenon*, "that which appears or is seen," noun use of neuter present participle of *phainesthai*, "to appear," passive of *phainein*, "bring to light, cause to appear, show" (from PIE root *bha-* (1), "to shine"). Meaning "extraordinary occurrence" first recorded 1771. Plural is *phenomena*.

NOMINAL

Through the bare branch, a flutter.

I thought a flag was an immense wing.

Sky sliced through with long clouds.

The city is an avalanche; all torn down.

I have a bridge in mind; a river.

River, clouds, sky, wing, branch.

Flag. City. Avalanche. Bridge. Mind.

WOUNDED EVIDENCE

"Capitalism cannot reform itself; it is doomed to self-destruction. No universal selfishness can bring social good to all."

—*W. E. B. Du Bois*

1.

In a quadrant of the adored city   acid green warning

asphalt heat and the team's mandate

to punish without call to win all our voices

under the sweet hues of belief

mask of the infidel and the politics of

the unlike

        fastened to the gate

           not to swerve not to include
               the plural nomenclature   the bright fallacy of

        belonging and as if

to get under the skin of the crowd
to wrestle the increment
into being

        to vow as
      the essay has lost its way
thin pages
torn   raining scraps
      little *the* little *this*

wounded evidence.

2.

The scene cannot rescue the pilgrim.

She's wandered off in her

slippers and vest

across the arroyo's hot, pathless sand.

She will return to the module of the dump

with its incoherent grace, its

daisies and cracked blue glass.

Her search will yield

an ecstatic find, the rapture

of a refrain. Sing! Sing!

And into her open mouth

pours a landscape of fields and apples,

pastures and rivers, hills and lakes,

the damp underside of a rabbit, or fox.

3.

Look! World, rim laden,

flooding over lastingness—its cup, its spill,

the untraveled and the doubling

architecture's image, down there, puddled

repeat of the next appearance,

after counting, and the *I am* is not,

barely recollected, voice coiling

into the drain,

with its hair and grounds,

stones visible between hemlocks,

unmarked, as in a bin,

one among many, among

forbidden procedures

filed away, or sealed, like lips.

4.

Irregular parable of the unconsidered.

The sanctioned she,

her adamancy, and rich

rewards for her club of fans.

The acolytes of glamour.

The followers of the mask.

These are notes

from an earlier procedure

that involved pain from one to ten.

Difficult to believe we are living now.

Difficult to believe it all hasn't

been snatched back

into gas and dust

arcing across the universe

soundlessly. *Does sound*

disappear? Roberto asked.

That's a mixed metaphor, he said,

and I had to think, sipping my coffee.

Seeing is not believing.

Hearing is not appearing.

5.

The collection of Walter Benjamin's

essays on Charles Baudelaire

carries the subtitle "A Lyric Poet

in the Era of High Capitalism,"

or that is how it is translated

by Harry Zohn in my Verso

edition, from 1983, although

the essays were first published

in 1969. These bits of bibliographical

information are given here

because I was wondering if this subtitle

is a reference to Adorno's famous remark

to write lyric poetry after Auschwitz is barbaric,

and if the relation of lyric poetry

to the horrors of Auschwitz

and to high capitalism

is different in kind.

When did Benjamin

write these essays, and

when did Adorno make his remark?

My other wonder is

what to call this present moment,

especially as I have been

thinking, after the summer's

events, which included the Brexit vote,

the nomination of Donald J. Trump

as the Republican Party's presidential candidate,

and an almost constant eruption of violence—bombings, shootings—

I have been thinking that we are all now

included in the precariat, those

who have no standing, no place to stand,

rootless as Milton's exiled angels

plummeting through space.

And I have been thinking, also,

that the coupling of capitalism

with democracy,

that assumed marriage

in the West, seems

to be coming undone, that

the machinery of global capital

is no longer aligned with

the aspirations of democratic ideals,

at least as found, founded

in America. Our

political class, our *leaders*,

seem not to distinguish between

these ideas, the one

of political discourse, the other

economic. If Benjamin

was writing about "high capitalism"

as the epithet for Baudelaire's nineteenth-century Paris,

what are we to call ours, now? *Late capitalism* seems as

lame as *postmodernism*, both

signs that language has defaulted

and that our capacity

to actually see or

understand our present

moment is, for lack of a better word,

impoverished. What does

"lyric poetry" have to do with it?

6.

Two of Claudia Rankine's books,

Don't Let Me Be Lonely

and her acclaimed 2014 *Citizen*, carry

the subtitle "An American Lyric,"

with evident purpose or intention to

draw her readers' attention to the word

lyric as noun, not adjective.

Her poems are not *lyrical*.

If these great books are

lyrics, who writes or wrote

their tunes? This is not an entirely

facetious or disingenuous

question, since

I think the answer might be

relevant to my misgivings.

Songs. I sometimes

believe America

depends on,

is held together by,

songs more than any other medium,

and then I want to believe

also that it is less easy to turn

a song into a commodity

than, say, a painting,

although, as we know,

the singer of the song is another matter

even if she does her best to

subvert or resist the

transformation of her person

into a thing.

7.

Our appetites shoved things aside,

pushed them

into the aisle, where they

turned to acid, which the children,

believing in magical elixirs, drink

to keep from becoming man-woman

but, instead, transform

into great beasts

lumbering over the landscape,

bigger than dinosaurs or alligators or elephants,

bigger than the warships in the harbor,

than the jet overhead; bigger,

even, than the moon. Let's play

drink the acid green and kill everything in our way,

they call, racing up and down Main Street.

to Roberto Tejada

—I write against an undertow today, but I will not just now reveal its cause, only that it is tugging me backward. Meanwhile, I am reading an account of the *Annunciation*, by Fra Angelico (one of the frescoes in the cells of the Convent of San Marco, Florence, from c. 1440), by the art historian Georges Didi-Huberman, in his book *Confronting Images*, from 1990. He offers ways of encountering an art object that might be applied to how we approach the reading of some poems. He speaks about an "incomplete semiology" consisting of "the visible, the legible, and the invisible," a tripartite "set" circumscribing or framing ideas of knowledge which, he says, are essentially derived from Kant. He speaks about Freud as a counter to Kant—in particular, Freud's invention of the Subject in relation to knowledge; he mentions symptoms, repetition, distortion, and, finally, the idea of a "retrospective revision" given to the psyche's figuring of knowledge. He says that the figural is under "the tyranny of the legible." All this leads to an astonishing claim:

> *There is, however, an alternative to this incomplete semiology. It is based on the general hypothesis that the efficacy of these images is not due solely to the trans-mission of knowledge—visible, legible, or invisible—but that, on the contrary, their efficacy operates constantly in the intertwinings, even the imbroglio, of transmitted and dismantled knowledges, of produced and transformed not-knowledges. It requires, then, a gaze that would not draw close only to discern and recognize, to name what it grasps at any cost—but would, first, distance itself a bit and abstain from clarifying everything immediately. Something like a suspended attention, a prolonged suspension of the moment of reaching conclu-sions, where interpretation would have time to deploy itself in several dimen-sions, between the grasped visible and the lived ordeal of a relinquishment. There would also be, in this alternative, a dialectical moment—surely unthink-able in positivist terms—consisting of not-grasping the image, of letting oneself be grasped by it instead: thus of letting go of one's knowledge about it.*

—As I am dependent on a sense of light, or sight, I would like you to tell why this passage so excites you.

—I will try. Maybe everything I have been writing is engaged with this interrogation of the relation between seeing and saying, visibility and legibility, as filtered through Didi-Huberman's sense of suspension, where "not-knowledge" is felt in a pause, a gaze; where verbal language does not lay immediate claim to what is perceived, an equation I have sometimes called, dumbly, "this is this." As if all possible encounters with the phenomenal world could find words.

—Well, I am certainly glad when I make people speechless with amazement.

—Speechless, but reaching instantly for their camera phones. Such silence, such awe, is not the same as "the lived ordeal of a relinquishment," which forms around the suspended moment, the resistance to definition by verbal means which seems to me a grim empiricism.

—Are we heading into Wittgenstein's famous remark, the one about remaining silent in the face of the unsayable?

—Maybe, but maybe not. I think *this* silence is full, replete, where interpretation is suspended into "several dimensions." It's this dynamic that excites me. It feels architectural. In fact, this passage from Didi-Huberman is from the part of the book in which he is addressing the mystery of the "empty" space in the Fra Angelico fresco, the curved arch, reiterated in his drawing, of the convent's cell walls. Without allowing this "blank" space to fill with our gaze, we cannot possibly know—or, better, receive—the meaning of the *Annunciation*.

—This is a bit creepy, all this ecclesiastic stuff. Are you becoming religious?

—Don't be contemptuous. No, I have no religion. But I want our world—or maybe my world—not to be stripped entirely of wonder.

wonder (n.)

Old English *wundor*, "marvelous thing, miracle, object of astonishment," from Proto-Germanic **wundran* (source also of Old Saxon *wundar*,

Middle Dutch and Dutch *wonder*, Old High German *wuntar*, German *wunder*, Old Norse *undr*), of unknown origin. In Middle English it also came to mean the emotion associated with such a sight (late 13c.). To be *no wonder* was in Old English. The original *wonder drug* (1939) was Sulfanilamide.

wonder (v.)

Old English *wundrian*, "be astonished," also "admire; make wonderful, magnify," from the source of *wonder* (n.). Cognate with Dutch *wonderen*, Old High German *wuntaron*, German *wundern*. Sense of "entertain some doubt or curiosity" is late 13c. Related: *Wondered*; **wondering**.

Reflexive use (It wonders me that "I wonder why . . .") was common in Middle English and as late as Tindale (1533), and is said to survive in Yorkshire/Lincolnshire. In Pennsylvania German areas it is idiomatic from German *das wundert mich*.

THROWN

The world's mischief: ludicrous,

spent, or just hard. There is

a cry you will hear

after the final episode's

simple gesture. *What was that?*

Something crosses the line

just as night comes down,

not unprecedented, not

unkind, down

the way any above comes

down, as a stone

cast from a cloud into

an open palm.

Is it cruel, this

stone? It is an instant

overcome by falling, but

night is an event that lacks

the dumb volition of a stone.

The cry moves on.

SYMPTOM

Some star

sickens away from its *the*.

An unoriginal

contagion weighs down, not so much

falling as suffering

toward the mundane, like a crust of snow

becoming brackish mud. We're

anointed by these vagaries and their

iconographic slights

as we peer into the initialed surface

of a gorgeous blank, as if to discover

metonymy's touch. The field

blinks between shadow and

radiance, or between the dream

and what we might perceive as we rush

toward the ditch. Everything slated,

ambitions of a girl

visible for miles, her smiling aperture

and her lists, her vague hair

tossed, her arms reaching for fire.

At the window, a man peers in

as her brilliant fingers ignite the trees.

to Sophie Strand

MOWER

—Evening! Night's spidery spin is once again in view.

—Yes, I know.

—It glistens minutely.

—While I just descend into a whitish pale drape accompanied by your neighbor's incessant mowing, which compromises my calm passage.

—Yes. It's a morbid sound, the mower.

—Why morbid?

—Just antithetical to the actual moment's trace, so it has a deathly quality. Maybe this is how I think about all machines. The uninflected drone is unlike any natural sound, any voice, even the most rhythmic and methodical, like that of a bird or the infinite pulse of the sea.

—O, the sea.

—It's been a long time since I've been at or near the sea.

—Happily, I am at the sea simultaneously with being here with you.

—Yes, I know. You get around.

mower (n.)

Early 14c., agent noun from *mow* (v.). Mechanical sense is from 1852.

EARTH

—Good morning, Evening.

—What now?

—Now I'm having another one of those episodes in which dying seems very near.

—You seem to want to speak to me at these times.

—That's true. I am sorry; it must be tedious for you.

—Well, not really, as I am myself always ending. I just don't lament. What has brought you this time?

—I've been doing a lot of pruning of shrubs, and I have been reading Robert Pogue Harrison's *The Dominion of the Dead*.

—That might explain your mood.

—Possibly, although I think I reached for it because of the mood, rather than the other way around. I've been thinking about ideas of survival. What survives? *Sur-* must mean beyond or after: *beyond life*. Anyway, we are always reading about recovered writers whose work was barely known in life and then, or now, after death, they are rediscovered and republished; they have survived; they have an afterlife. This just happened with Lucia Berlin. My friend Kenward Elmslie was a fan and friend of hers; he read me snippets from her letters to him. Now a collection of her stories has been published to appreciative reviews. Anyway, Harrison talks eloquently about the earth as the *element* of our survival after death; its materiality allows for our life's inscription. He connects writing, or literature, to this aspect of earthliness. So:

> *In giving voice to the wound of mortality itself, literature houses or gives a home to even the most desolate kinds of grief. It gives us* back *that which we keep on losing, namely a cognizance or recognizance of our passionate and mortal natures. Hence the intrinsically posthumous character of the literary voice. . . . Works of literature, then, are more than enduring tablets where an author's words survive his or her demise. They are the gifts of human worlds,*

cosmic in nature, that hold their place in time so that the living and the unborn may inhabit them at will, make themselves at home in their articulate humanity—all thanks to the ultimate gift of the earth, which renders their testaments possible.

—Well, that's quite grand, isn't it? He wants to affix time to the materiality of space through the literary; he wants the past to be held there in perpetuity. I'm incapable of knowing what that is like, being always and only passage.

—It's funny how the word for you is a noun, which *is* a thing: *evening*. And then there is that adjective, *crepuscular,* which sounds like a skin disease. I can't imagine how it came to describe you; I suppose I have to look at the etymology to find out.

—You do that.

—The noun problem is related to the fact problem.

—You need to be more precise.

—Nouns seem to refer to material objects; facts seem also to be object-like. I know this is simplistic, and not quite true, since there are all those nouns that refer to abstractions.

—Like *abstraction*?

—Or, as I think we just mentioned, *evening*.

—I am not an abstraction.

—Yes, as we have established, you are a phenomenon. And I don't know why I keep thinking of facts as thing-like, because they aren't. I guess I want them to have a kind of permanence, a reliable fixity in our new era of *fake news*, a linguistic paradox if ever there was one. Anyway, I've been reading another book, *The Mind in the Cave*; it's about the so-called *prehistoric* cave paintings that, I am thinking now, are congruent with Pogue Harrison's argument about material inscription and a need for humans to mark our presence on earth. It's a strange idea, isn't it?

—It is for me.

earth (n.)

Old English *eorþe*, "ground, soil, dirt, dry land; country, district," also used (along with *middangeard*) for "the (material) world, the abode of man" (as opposed to the heavens or the underworld), from Proto-Germanic **ertho** (source also of Old Frisian *erthe*, "earth," Old Saxon *ertha*, Old Norse *jörð*, Middle Dutch *eerde*, Dutch *aarde*, Old High German *erda*, German *Erde*, Gothic *airþa*), from extended form of PIE root **er-** (2) "earth, ground." The earth considered as a planet was so called from c. 1400. Use in old chemistry is from 1728. *Earth-mover*, "large digging machine," is from 1940.

VALUE

1.

You might find a better joy outside the cave

    noun drenched

               our sacrificial stone

           you could walk uneasily toward that blue

        indoctrination

        and the lifted motion

  s   stranded

      lamb   a better joy

    in the weirdness of the sweater   the late *noir*

coming this close   last instance of the first encounter

coming this close to   rudimentary adhesion

and the classical removal from the cloud

sainted apparition

    clinging to pitch

  to the prior image

and the segue   dearest forethought

the bridge and the hall

the acquisitive glamour of autumnal tide

where   if the sun

      were to travel low and low across the schoolroom

          and you were to ask, *do you know? what is this?*

delivered through architectural limbs

          scrappy talismans of the unsaid   adrift

as if you could see only what you wish for

in the eternal foreground

hero returned from his journey

his feet forever wet

or recall the dream

where mother calls you on the phone

sister unweds her father

    your lover

          adrift among the vagrancy of nouns

the intersection   hope's violence

agitated

                    intolerable timing of the muscle

                    hitched up

to the excluded ship

crossing woven borders

hay drying under the August sun

          windrows curled and the lament of the swing

                    the low, the chariot

             ropes taut under the August sun

                    what noise raptured

                         what cauldron of dark light

vulgar forfeiture   into the abrasive toll.

2.

And so to come into the acrid avenue

and look down:

                    things flung into the bushes

bottles and such

the hidden addendum awash in oil

the boy in his grave,

the untranslatable sex.

This is the list that morning endures.

In the near distance, a tree is shedding gold,

this is how it is, this is

not the simple street, its mobile portrait tomb.

Girl, under the wet earth,

collecting dues, counting and counting

as the curator

treads at the water's edge.

Bring me silvers, bring me rubies, bring me

buckets of diamonds in ice.

No one wakes without loss.

3.

I understand. You want facts.

You want writing about exchange

and use and Egypt's plight. You want

unthwarted descriptions of

empire and history; quotations from

Lincoln and Douglas,

quatrains of indelible

sound for transcription into

the instrument you hold

in your hand for company.

You want to be told.

I'm tellin' you! our

housekeeper, Cora

Brown,

exclaimed often.

I remember Stalin lying

dead on the

front page and the killing of

Emmett Till. Frederick

Douglass was named,

later,

after he could read

and was free,

for a character

in Sir Walter Scott's poem

The Lady of the Lake,

but you already knew that.

He, Douglass, added the extra *s,*

so that a mirror

or window occurs: *glass.*

My cousin Douglas

with one *s*

died when he was twelve

of cystic fibrosis.

Liz, Katie, and Matthew

followed suit.

to Michael Carlebach

VISTA

Thought's mimetic ghost
quells appearance
even as the race to the finish
seems to fly before the eye's
retrospective gaze. Regard me,
says the invading shimmer,
the head of a raven,
the anointed air of a sudden storm,
regard me, as I cast my domain
before you

and find, in the rhythms of the same,
an absentee link, air in the pipes,
stains on the arm of the chair,
embellishments
among the retirees
on their bicycles, singing
downhill as the drawing nears
completion.

LIGHT

—Evening! There are times when you cast such an extraordinary light, it makes me want to hold on to it and give it away to strangers. I've taken so many photographs just as the sun flares out from a low horizontal, casting its sheen so the greens are amplified and the shadows darken, and all the colors in the garden take on augmented radiance.

—Thank you.

—I'm writing this while I'm thinking of a small still-life painting by Chardin, *Seville Orange, Silver Goblet, Apples, Pear, and Two Bottles* (1750), I saw a few days ago at the Metropolitan Museum of Art in New York. Evidently this painting has not ever been in a public space; it has spent its life in private hands. But the person who owns it has lent it to the Met while she is away, and so there it is for all to see. A work of such tender, acute attention to how light touches materials of differing opacities, densities, colors: skin of an apple or pear, glass bottle, silver goblet, placed together on a thick stone table, its edge duplicating the picture plane, emphasizing the illusion of material gravity.

—I do that most days—touch objects on your table, the candlesticks and flowers.

—Yes, and I love it when you do. And in the painting, it is not so much the objects we recognize as the way the light—*your light!*—enters from the picture's left, and caresses each surface with a quickened, radiant bloom. How long did it take Chardin to paint this picture? Did he wait patiently each day for the autumnal light to enter, brushes readied for his palette of oil paint? This is what a photographer would do, but a painter must have a different kind of patience, to anoint time's luminous movement with paint: wet, dry, wet. Was he partly observing, partly recollecting? Glass and metal, fruit and table, each receiving the light differently, and so its effects are distributed across the picture plane, a kind of illuminated wind made manifest, held, forever transfixed.

to Stephan Wolohojian

light (adj.1)

"not heavy, having little actual weight," from Old English *leoht* (West Saxon), *leht* (Anglian), "not heavy, light in weight; lightly constructed; easy to do, trifling; quick, agile," also of food, sleep, etc., from Proto-Germanic **lingkhtaz* (source also of Old Norse *lettr*, Swedish *lätt*, Old Frisian, Middle Dutch *licht*, German *leicht*, Gothic *leihts*), from PIE root ***legwh-** "not heavy, having little weight." The adverb is Old English *leohte*, from the adjective.

Meaning "frivolous" is from early 13c.; that of "unchaste" from late 14c., both from the notion of "lacking moral gravity" (compare **levity**). Of literature from 1590s. *Light industry* (1919) makes use of relatively lightweight materials. The notion in *make light of* (1520s) is "unimportance." Alternative spelling *lite*, the darling of advertisers, is first recorded 1962. *Light horse* "light armed cavalry" is from 1530s. *Light-skirts* "woman of easy virtue" is attested from 1590s. *Lighter-than-air* (adj.) is from 1887.

light (adj.2)

"not dark," Old English *leoht* (West Saxon), *leht* (Anglian), "luminous, bright, beautiful, shining; having much light," common Germanic (cognates: Old Saxon and Old High German *lioht*, Old Frisian *liacht*, German *licht* "bright"), from the source of Old English *leoht* (see **light** (n.)). Meaning "pale-hued" is from 1540s; prefixed to other color adjectives from early 15c. In earlier Middle English in reference to colors it meant "bright, vivid" (early 14c.).

light (n.)

"brightness, radiant energy, that which makes things visible," Old English *leht* (Anglian), *leoht* (West Saxon), "light, daylight; spiritual illumination," from Proto-Germanic **leukhtam* (source also of Old Saxon *lioht*, Old Frisian *liacht*, Middle Dutch *lucht*, Dutch *licht*, Old High German *lioht*, German *Licht*, Gothic *liuhaþ* "light"), from PIE root ***leuk-** "light, brightness."

The *-gh-* was an Anglo-French scribal attempt to render the Germanic hard *-h-* sound, which has since disappeared from this word. The figurative spiritual sense was in Old English; the sense of "mental illumination" is first recorded mid-15c. Meaning "something used for igniting" is from 1680s. Meaning "a consideration which puts something in a certain view" (as in *in light of*) is from 1680s. Short for *traffic light* from 1938.

Quaker use is by 1650s; *New Light/Old Light* in church doctrine also is from 1650s. Meaning "person eminent or conspicuous" is from 1590s. A source of joy or delight has been the *light of (someone's) eyes* since Old English:

Ðu eart dohtor min, minra eagna leoht [Juliana].

Phrases such as *according to (one's) lights* "to the best of one's natural or acquired capacities" preserve an older sense attested from 1520s. To figuratively *stand in (someone's) light* is from late 14c. To *see the light* "come into the world" is from 1680s; later as "come to full realization" (1812). The rock concert *light-show* is from 1966. To be *out like a light* "suddenly or completely unconscious" is from 1934.

light (v.1)

"to touch down," as a bird from flight, "get down or descend," as a person from horseback, from Old English *lihtan* "to alight; to alleviate, make less heavy," from Proto-Germanic *linkhtijan, literally "to make light," from *lingkhtaz "not heavy" (see **light** (adj.1)). Apparently the etymological sense is "to dismount" (a horse, etc.), and thus relieve it of one's weight."

Alight has become the more usual word. To *light on* "happen upon, come upon" is from late 15c. To *light out* "leave hastily, decamp" is 1866, from a nautical meaning "move out, move heavy objects" (1841), a word of unknown origin but perhaps belonging to this word (compare **lighter** (n.1)).

light (v.2)

"to shed light; to set on fire," late Old English *lihtan* (Anglian), *liehtan* (West Saxon), originally transitive, "to ignite, set on fire," also in a spiritual sense, "to illuminate, fill with brightness." It is common Germanic (cognates: Old Saxon *liohtian*, Old High German *liuhtan*, German *leuchten*, Gothic *liuhtjan* "to light"), from the source of **light** (n.).

Meaning "furnish light for" is from c. 1200; sense of "emit light, shed light, shine" is from c. 1300. Buck writes that *light* is "much more common than *kindle* even with fire, and only *light*, not *kindle*, with candle, lamp, pipe, etc." To *light up* is from c. 1200 as "give light to" (a room, etc.); 1861 in reference to a pipe, cigar, etc. Related: *Lighted*; **lighting**.

UNBELIEF, SEEING

1.

Yellow fortifies the drone's
       flared assertions, as of wind.

Redeemed from an old file,
       misnomers flee to attic dust.

Habitus of software: unroofed palace,
       leaked oil, etymology

French and distributed across
       the site's icon and partial

song. Hemlock shade. Open mouth
       stuck in the modem's blinking pulse.

An adventure among
       particulars, none of them recalled,

as if *sorrow could take one abroad,*
       away from the recluse harbor.

2.

Forfeiture at the gates: the merry
widow, the wise fool. O dearest

clone, put on your hat and shoes,
make your slow way across the rug.

What remains?
The soldiers have left

the field. The students are
in the building. Fires are set.

Our Lady of Masks is about to visit,
white gloves drawn over dark nails.

Our Lady of Dread is casting her vote,
hair a pale shimmer

in spring rain. Humming, she
counts her pennies and the dead.

3.

The crows are indifferent

but urgent.
The heron lopes

across a blowsy sky,

west to east,
seemingly enchanted

with itself.

An aristocratic bird, in

Plato's terms: noble
and graceful.

A boat is wheeled
down to the river.

The stones are
indifferent. Also the grass.

The bathers became paint.
The paint points

forward to a boy
wearing a black shirt with letters.

The letters are indifferent.
A girl reads the words on the shirt.

to Willa

THREAD

(Note: The italicized phrases in parts 2 and 3 refer to titles of books.)

1.

Spool of dark-green thread rolls slowly backward onto a daisy field

not found unwinding downhill

most narrow path

term of the unmended

darker than grass

fabricated

the pit of a plum

damp headless rabbit

tune-stripped air

some

murderous repeat

preselects the abrasive

& now

all implication

swelters diaristically

O my small

Lord.

Please provide

an alabaster form

to ruse the system.

Am ambient

am docile

among contractions

also I am

an integer of false claims

as if that drawing

were by my own hand.

So speaketh away

from adulation, its

syntactical shape

already fate's tightest knot.

How the machine

hates an anomaly,

how it abuses imperfection.

2.

Meanwhile

confidence swells

across the aperture of

singularity whose

mode is infinite starlight

and her own pleasures,

dream swept up

onto a ladder, climbing

toward the voice

you may have known.

Beloved swims in a pond

reflecting the constellated

grief of centuries,

monks gathered

around the bier of Saint Francis,

walls sweat

where later a sacred fount

beckons the oldest awe

into its stainless basin

and in the night a girl

writes words

in colored chalk

on the pavement stone.

Every force evolves a form.

And the petals of a rose

have fallen

into partial pinks

and collapsed browns

as if soiled or bruised

and the cicadas have gone back

into the underworld, webbed

wings strewn, red eyes blind.

The dream has left me

bewildered. My neighbor's

dog barked it open and out

I fell into the milky dawn,

into *the practice of everyday life.*

3.

Were we to return

the covers would open

and the sheets

introduce us to a

sentence drawn from Spinoza, he

who spoke of a third kind of

knowledge, and my legs

would wrap around your body

in *the poetics of space.* This

would occur *after the end*

after *the sense of sight,*

after the apocalypse and

all the words we lived

among. You would describe

the art of interference

and I would argue for

the will to believe, all this

before our morning coffee

set on a small table

in the field

not far from a stream

where a mockingbird

shapes time

above the threaded grass.

4.

A spider has netted the air.

This comes in a kit. Seeds

also available: see below.

Blissed out on the sea's

dragnet, war fires

extinguished,

and so candles

lit for the drowned,

many but

not all

accounted.

The arch

has collapsed,

singers departed.

Thread pulls

at the flat

horizon

agitating the hour.

The salty

cauldron of the Nile

rubs into our wounds—crusty

palimpsest of the profile frieze.

5.

To go out from the city, find

a path to install

on the wall where the sun,

ever full, distributes

plenitude, and its agents,

Grace, Levity, and Chance.

Let them beget

new justice

into our dithering trials.

All along the edges

there are crude blue margins,

fists of brown leaves.

A mask floats above,

buoyant and empty.

Ya, ya, says bird, leaving the yard.

Voice recedes into eternity's

pale marker. A

video shows

replications of figures

crowded onto rectangles,

a choir of ravenous

beetles felling the trees.

6.

Blind slippage in the unanchored field.

That protein assemblage is

taut among least vibrations.

This inner song had best abate, lest

all achieve stasis

around a melancholy pall, our

beings' repeated

inferences, and the lyric joys

hinge inclusivity

onto the aesthetic dump

where our hopes

flip for breathable air

at all our thresholds:

glass, door, cup,

the books and the fabric,

the ever-spiraling list

traced away from duration

to install the silent archive.

to Ann Hamilton

WEED

Girl is thinking to plant a snow fountain

to cool her dreams

and to divest their triple narratives, dawn

after dawn. Who are these persons

staggering from bed to bed,

wearing hats from another time, desire

from another time. Once it starts

it can't stop. The mountain arc is remnant,

immobile as a drawing

by the hand of a master. Maybe it's

always a matter of double entendre,

although the violins have quit and she is tired

of the evening song's incessant

refrain. Girl is thinking to plant

her heart in the coarse mud along the road

to see if it grows an imitation weed heart.

The taut elbow of the branch

is starkly imminent,

nothing to do with what girl has been

dreaming recently. A fistful of

buds at the end of a stem. Words

could be listed but the list

is unearned, a dusty syllabus

in the stacks. Girl watches

as the evening, its angle

slanting up from the river,

litters the air with particulars.

THINK

—Why do you like to read so many abstruse authors? I sense it isn't very good for your psyche—nor for your poems, for that matter.

—You are probably right. Coleridge asks himself somewhere if he thinks too much to be a poet. I don't quite know what the answer is. I have always liked essays that move freely through and around a subject, and I like how poets write about things other than poetry—visual art, for example—as well as about poetics. Poets need to know about things other than poems. I like the thought of poems and prose essays bleeding into each other, cognition flowing into sensuous apprehension and perception—experience—and the other way around, all in the service of enlarging the purview or changing, however slightly, reality. This ambition entices me to not live so strictly within the categorical. Sometimes I think poetry is an orphan wanderer, and I am attempting to house and nourish it.

—These seem like generic reasons. I wanted something more personal.

—Oh, I see. I think I am in search of foundation, or ground. I'm porous to impulses and reactive to events. I often feel without anchor or foothold in the world. I like to read things that might quell some of this uncertainty, not exactly by denying it, but rather by giving it a reason to be as it is. Does that make sense?

—You read for a rationale?

—No, not a rationale; for support, and for absorption into a matrix of thinking about thought itself, a quest of a kind: to know how or if thought, when it is expressed in written language, bears a relation to the activity of worldness, or being in the world. I seem especially to love the kind of thought—Emerson's, for example—that doesn't know where it is going; this excites me, getting lost in order to find.

—Still, I feel you are avoiding something here.

—You don't normally press me so.

—Well, something is at stake, because of course these texts signal a certain intellectual grandiosity and pretension—a certain *elitism*, in the current phrase—and I think it's important for you to reckon with this fact.

—Yes, I know. Recently, I was having a conversation with some folks who wanted to know something about my process. I was asked about my reading habits, and I said I read a lot of abstract, philosophical authors. One of the persons in the room glared at me with indignation and asked, "Are you a thinker?" I felt it as an accusation.

—What did you say?

—I said that Hannah Arendt believed that thoughtlessness is a form of evil. She wrote, "Violence begins where speech ends."

—Hmm. So then thinking is a form of good? Are you trying to be good?

—Yes, I guess, but I am also wanting to get under the surface of things, to feel less bewildered by these times, less forsaken. I want to know if a person—if I—can arrive at some peace of mind by simply continuing to pursue possibilities and not be thwarted by a sense that there is nothing to be done. The events of our time seem so capricious, unfounded in consensus or deep structures. I am not an optimist, but I do think hope is important.

—Another tarnished word.

—When I was younger, I liked to throw the I Ching, the Chinese Book of Changes. It was a fad then. I was wanting something or someone to tell me not only who I was but how I should go on. I loved the sense that a chance operation could reveal some direction hidden from plain view; I loved the phrase "It furthers one to cross the great waters." One of my favorite hexagrams was called, I think, "Innocence (The Unexpected)." This about sums up my state of mind: to come to something without prior judgment, fresh, and enter the unexpected not with fear but gladness.

—Then you read in order to believe that thinking will open possibilities into the unknown?

—Something like that. I suppose it is why I continue to love and admire many modernist artists and writers, their ambition, not for themselves but for work; their sense that cognition and imagination are conjoined, twinned, not dualistic, not capable of being reduced to formulaic academic categories or special genres, nor yet sold to the highest bidder. Their ferocity in the face of intractable historical misery, their determination to find forms to meet the wreckage and depletion and terror head-on, and with these forms to redeem the human, at least in part.

—The old idea: *We have art in order not to perish of the truth.*

—Yes, that line from Nietzsche I pasted into one of my first journals. But what about now, when "the truth" itself has become a kind of waif, unanchored and adrift in a *sea of opinion* crawling with mindless creatures? I guess I am really speaking about my belief that art is still and always essential to the human conversation, to our sense of connectivity, our capacity to imagine that we can make things better, not necessarily in the sense of progress, but in relation to making meaning happen now. Art helps us to recognize and celebrate our differences within some fundamental likeness. Yet contemporary art-making feels impoverished— driven by immediacies, yes, but determined by concerns outside of the act of imaginative creation. Well, now you see what you've done. You've got me up on my preachy high horse, from which I am bound to fall.

think (v.)

Old English *þencan*, "imagine, conceive in the mind; consider, meditate, remember; intend, wish, desire" (past tense *þohte*, past participle *geþoht*), probably originally "cause to appear to oneself," from Proto-Germanic *thankjan* (source also of Old Frisian *thinka*, Old Saxon *thenkian*, Old High German *denchen*, German *denken*, Old Norse *þekkja*, Gothic *þagkjan*).

Old English *þencan* is the causative form of the distinct Old English verb *þyncan*, "to seem, to appear" (past tense *þuhte*, past participle *geþuht*), from Proto-Germanic *thunkjan* (source also of German *dünken*, *däuchte*). Both are from PIE *tong-*, "to think, feel," which also is the root of **thought** and **thank**.

The two Old English words converged in Middle English and *þyncan*, "to seem," was absorbed, except for its preservation in archaic **methinks**, "it seems to me." As a noun, "act of prolonged thinking," from 1834. The figurative *thinking cap* is attested from 1839.

SOME OF US

See others of us. Some of us kiss others of us. Some of us

have left home and believe in the commerce of belief

and that writing will save some of us from harm and

believe there must be a pony somewhere

and some of us turn and turn again toward the fire

and have fallen suddenly in front of some of us while

the man-clown comes down the aisle

and our elders cannot smile

even as there are words to comfort some of us

and not others, not others

sitting in the rags of our life

or writing to get us anywhere else while

some of us stand like statues at noon

imagining ourselves as history and some disapprove

of all things happy and glad

and some of us are always hungry

and some of us are always happy and glad

and some of us believe in witches

and some of us cannot follow along the route but

stay pinioned and alert having killed the beautiful

beasts of the field, having waited for kingdom come,

having flexed and watched and searched

and taught and shown how some of us are joyful

and some not, scribbling our tunes on the wall,

some of us are perplexed among stones

and some of us have disappeared

into the great conversation

of being, its white light of shipwreck,

and some of us are bored too soon

and others of us are beyond salvation

and some of us stare into hope

and smile

and prepare for the worst

and are radiant among machines and graves

and are radiant in the meadow

while some of us travel and some of us stand watch

as if we could reap

as if there were no weathers to impede

nor impassible routes and some of us

hate others of us

and some of us are easy and aloof

and some are lost in a crowd

or are always wanting more and some of us shout

and some of us are just passing by others of us

and want to remember

this or that song.

AWE

—Hello, Evening.

—Hi.

—We are coming to the end of our conversation for the time being.

—That's an odd turn of phrase, *for the time being*.

—I guess it's an idiom, although I always think of W. H. Auden, who called his long Christmas Oratorio by that name.

—And what do you think it means? From my point of view, it is cumbersome and redundant, as isn't everything always *for the time being*?

—I suppose, but there is some other layer, or layers, of meaning, as so often in language, so it doesn't quite work to think of it as a single; the phrase has resonance, like a chord in music.

—O well, you know I am not very good at these kinds of elaborations. I think you are always straining toward something high-toned, and it competes with another urge toward plainness.

—That's perceptive. This tug happens in a number of venues: décor, dress, poetics. I often feel a powerful desire for elaboration, for texture and nuance, a kind of complex maximalism, which pulls against a desire for simplicity and the clarity it can bring.

—You want to be eloquent but clear. Contemporary but universal.

—I guess. I think I fear being too easily reductive. My mother used to tell me to *dress for style not for fashion* and I think this became a kind of irresolute dilemma: how to have both? Eloquence is reassuring in its illusions, like certain modes of classical music—Bach, most particularly—or the poetry of Wallace Stevens: *Perhaps it gives / In the universal intercourse*. Stevens avows the workings of mind as it frets "things as they are": reality. He wonders if mind and reality are contiguous or separate: that old question. Wonder, in both senses, is the central issue. I think Arendt speaks about it in *The Human Condition*.

—I hear her name a lot these days.

—Yes, she is a frequent voice for those of us who are trying to find a way from the past to the future. Something I read of hers recently speaks about the loss of wonder in philosophy. The trouble with having a porous memory is that everything, details, citations, names, quickly dissolve and so only a trace is left. But look! Thanks to an unusually thorough index in her book, I find the passage. Arendt is talking about fabrication, about craft, in relation to "idea." She writes:

> *Historically, the source of this contemplation, which we find for the first time described in the Socratic school, is at least twofold. On the one hand, it stands in obvious and consistent connection with the famous contention of Plato, quoted by Aristotle, that* thaumazein, *the shocked wonder at the miracle of Being, is the beginning of all philosophy.*

—That's oddly exciting.
—Arendt goes on to speak about this "shocked wonder" as ultimately a state of "speechlessness"—this would, at least in one disposition, be awe, wouldn't it? She ends the paragraph: "*Theoria*, in fact, is only another word for *thaumazein*; the contemplation of truth at which the philosopher ultimately arrives is the philosophically purified speechless wonder with which he began."
—Well, you know, I am in favor of speechlessness. You humans should try it more often, awe or no awe.
—Last night a friend asked me if I thought Charles Olson had read Hannah Arendt. It's an interesting question and my guess is *no*, in part because I feel so strongly his, Olson's, essential misanthropic misogyny. My friend had asked because of Arendt's interest in *polis*, which is of course one of Olson's key words. So, in "Maximus to Gloucester, Letter 27 [withheld]":

There is no strict personal order

for my inheritance.

        No Greek will be able

to discriminate my body.

            An American

is a complex of occasions,

themselves a geometry

of spatial nature.

        I have this sense,

that I am one

with my skin

            Plus this—plus this:

that forever the geography

which leans in

on me I compell

backwards I compell Gloucester

to yield, to

change

            Polis

is this

—*Plus this* morphs into *polis is this.*

—And I am morphing into Night.

—Goodnight, Evening.

awe (n.)

c. 1300, *aue,* "fear, terror, great reverence," earlier *aghe,* c. 1200, from a Scandinavian source, such as Old Norse *agi,* "fright"; from Proto-Germanic **agiz-** (source also of Old English *ege,* "fear," Old High German *agiso,* "fright, terror," Gothic *agis,* "fear, anguish"), from PIE **agh-es-** (source also of Greek *akhos,* "pain, grief"), from root **agh-** (1) "to be depressed, be afraid" (see **ail**). Current sense of "dread mixed with admiration or veneration" is due to biblical use with reference to the Supreme Being. *To stand in awe* (early 15c.) originally was simply *to stand awe.* *Awe-inspiring* is recorded from 1814

THE POET

The poet turns, sky halted, awkward. The poet is arrested; the poet
rests. The resting poet watches the remaining sky. Sky fits into an empty
basket marked *the poem*. Sky papery, thinly lit by the bluish addendum
of day. The poet has a measure: day. The poet finds a stone. The poet
puts the stone into the empty basket marked *the poem* and collects up
the rest: day, sky, and sea, all variously held by a bluish addendum. The
wind empties the basket marked *the poem* of its stuff: stone, day, sea, sky.
The empty basket is light. Night falls. Night falls and the poet turns,
awkwardly, toward the released sea. The sea is encrypted. The poet
cannot read the sea. The poet hears the thwarted crescendo and places
that into the empty basket marked *the poem*. The basket churns heavily,
awkwardly, heaving with the sound of the illegible sea and the *that*.
The poet sees that something is missing from the bluish turning into
the arrested night sky, a missing that collapses into an addendum. The
arrested poet holds fast to the addendum. The basket marked *the poem*
rides out into the encrypted, unreadable sea.

spell (v.1)

Early 14c., "read letter by letter, write or say the letters of"; c. 1400, "form words by means of letters," apparently a French word that merged with or displaced a native Old English one; both are from the same Germanic root, but the French word had evolved a different sense. The native word is Old English *spellian*, "to tell, speak, discourse, talk," from Proto-Germanic **spellam* (source also of Old High German *spellon*, "to tell," Old Norse *spjalla*, Gothic *spillon*, "to talk, tell"), from PIE **spel-* (2), "to say aloud, recite."

But the current senses seem to come from Anglo-French *espeller*, Old French *espelir*, "mean, signify, explain, interpret," also "spell out letters, pronounce, recite," from Frankish **spellon*, "to tell," or some other Germanic source, ultimately identical with the native word.

Related: *spelled*; **spelling**. In early Middle English still "to speak, preach, talk, tell," hence such expressions as *hear spell*, "hear (something) told or talked about," *spell the wind*, "talk in vain" (both 15c.). Meaning "form words with proper letters" is from 1580s. *Spell out*, "explain step-by-step," is first recorded 1940, American English. Shakespeare has *spell (someone) backwards*, "reverse the character of, explain in a contrary sense, portray with determined negativity."

spell (n.1)

Old English *spell*, "story, saying, tale, history, narrative, fable; discourse, command," from Proto-Germanic **spellam* (see **spell (v.1)**). Compare Old Saxon *spel*, Old Norse *spjall*, Old High German *spel*, Gothic *spill*, "report, discourse, tale, fable, myth";

German *Beispiel*, "example." From c. 1200 as "an utterance, something said, a statement, remark"; meaning "set of words with supposed magical or occult powers, incantation, charm" first recorded 1570s; hence any means or cause of enchantment.

The term "spell" is generally used for magical procedures which cause harm, or force people to do something against their will— unlike charms for healing, protection, etc. [*Oxford Dictionary of English Folklore*]

Also in Old English, "doctrine; a sermon; religious instruction or teaching; the gospel; a book of the Bible"; compare **gospel**.

spell (v.2)

"Work in place of (another)," 1590s, earlier *spele*, from Old English *spelian*, "to take the place of, be substitute for, represent," related to *gespelia*, "substitute," of uncertain origin. Perhaps related to *spilian*, "to play" (see **spiel**). Related: *spelled*; **spelling**.

spell (n.2)

1620s, "a turn of work in place of another," from **spell** (v.2); compare Old English *gespelia*, "a substitute." Meaning shifted toward "continuous course of work" (1706), probably via notion of shift work (as at sea), where one man or crew regularly "spelled" another. Hence "continuous stretch" of something (weather, etc.), recorded by 1728. Hence also, via the notion in *give a spell* (1750), "relieve another by taking a turn of work," came the sense "interval of rest or relaxation" (1845), which took the word to a sense opposite what it had at the start.

MARINA VAN ZUYLEN

Poet and essayist Ann Lauterbach is the author of ten books of poetry and three books of essays, including *The Night Sky: Writings on the Poetics of Experience* and *The Given & The Chosen*; her 2009 poetry collection *Or to Begin Again* was a finalist for the National Book Award. She has written on the possible relation between poetics, aesthetics, and politics, as well as on the work of individual visual artists, including Cheyney Thompson and Kenji Fujita. She has taught critical writing at the School of Visual Arts in New York City, and was a visiting critic (sculpture) at Yale. Lauterbach's work has been recognized by fellowships from, among others, the Guggenheim Foundation and the John D. and Catherine T. MacArthur Foundation, and was the subject of a conference in Paris in 2015. She was awarded the annual Poetry Prize in 2017 from architect Steven Holl's "T" Space. She is the Ruth and David Schwab II Professor of Languages and Literature at Bard College, where she has been, since 1992, Co-Chair of Writing in Bard's multidiscipline MFA. A native of New York City, Lauterbach lives in Germantown, New York.

PENGUIN POETS

JOHN ASHBERY
Selected Poems
Self-Portrait in a Convex
  Mirror

PAUL BEATTY
Joker, Joker, Deuce

JOSHUA BENNETT
The Sobbing School

TED BERRIGAN
The Sonnets

LAUREN BERRY
The Lifting Dress

PHILIP BOOTH
Lifelines: Selected Poems
  1950–1999

JULIANNE BUCHSBAUM
The Apothecary's Heir

JIM CARROLL
Fear of Dreaming: The
  Selected Poems
Living at the Movies
Void of Course

ALISON HAWTHORNE DEMING
Genius Loci
Rope
Stairway to Heaven

CARL DENNIS
Another Reason
Callings
New and Selected Poems
  1974–2004
Night School
Practical Gods
Ranking the Wishes
Unknown Friends

DIANE DI PRIMA
Loba

STUART DISCHELL
Dig Safe

STEPHEN DOBYNS
Velocities: New and
  Selected Poems:
  1966–1992

EDWARD DORN
Way More West

ROGER FANNING
The Middle Ages

ADAM FOULDS
The Broken Word

CARRIE FOUNTAIN
Burn Lake
Instant Winner

AMY GERSTLER
Crown of Weeds
Dearest Creature
Ghost Girl
Medicine
Nerve Storm
Scattered at Sea

EUGENE GLORIA
Drivers at the Short-Time
  Motel
Hoodlum Birds
My Favorite Warlord

DEBORA GREGER
By Herself
Desert Fathers, Uranium
  Daughters
God
In Darwin's Room
Men, Women, and Ghosts
Western Art

TERRANCE HAYES
American Sonnets for
  My Past and Future
  Assassin
Hip Logic
How to Be Drawn
Lighthead
Wind in a Box

NATHAN HOKS
The Narrow Circle

ROBERT HUNTER
Sentinel and Other Poems

MARY KARR
Viper Rum

JACK KEROUAC
Book of Blues
Book of Haikus
Book of Sketches

JOANNA KLINK
Circadian
Excerpts from a Secret
  Prophecy
Raptus

JOANNE KYGER
As Ever: Selected Poems

ANN LAUTERBACH
Hum
If in Time: Selected Poems,
  1975–2000
On a Stair
Or to Begin Again
Spell
Under the Sign

CORINNE LEE
Plenty

PHILLIS LEVIN
May Day
Mercury
Mr. Memory & Other
  Poems

PATRICIA LOCKWOOD
Motherland Fatherland
  Homelandsexuals

WILLIAM LOGAN
Macbeth in Venice
Madame X
Rift of Light
Strange Flesh
The Whispering Gallery

J. MICHAEL MARTINEZ
Museum of the Americas

ADRIAN MATEJKA
The Big Smoke
Map to the Stars
Mixology

MICHAEL MCCLURE
Huge Dreams: San
  Francisco and Beat
  Poems

ROSE MCLARNEY
Its Day Being Gone

DAVID MELTZER
David's Copy: The Selected
  Poems of David Meltzer

ROBERT MORGAN
Dark Energy
Terroir

CAROL MUSKE-DUKES
Blue Rose
An Octave Above Thunder
Red Trousseau
Twin Cities

ALICE NOTLEY
Certain Magical Acts
Culture of One
The Descent of Alette
Disobedience
In the Pines
Mysteries of Small Houses

WILLIE PERDOMO
The Essential Hits of
  Shorty Bon Bon

LIA PURPURA
It Shouldn't Have Been
  Beautiful

LAWRENCE RAAB
The History of Forgetting
Visible Signs: New and
  Selected Poems

BARBARA RAS
The Last Skin
One Hidden Stuff

MICHAEL ROBBINS
Alien vs. Predator
The Second Sex

PATTIANN ROGERS
Generations
Holy Heathen Rhapsody
Quickening Fields
Wayfare

SAM SAX
Madness

ROBYN SCHIFF
A Woman of Property

WILLIAM STOBB
Absentia
Nervous Systems

TRYFON TOLIDES
An Almost Pure Empty
  Walking

SARAH VAP
Viability

ANNE WALDMAN
Gossamurmur
Kill or Cure
Manatee/Humanity
Structure of the World
  Compared to a Bubble
Trickster Feminism

JAMES WELCH
Riding the Earthboy 40

PHILIP WHALEN
Overtime: Selected Poems

ROBERT WRIGLEY
Anatomy of Melancholy
  and Other Poems
Beautiful Country
Box
Earthly Meditations: New
  and Selected Poems
Lives of the Animals
Reign of Snakes

MARK YAKICH
The Importance of Peeling
  Potatoes in Ukraine
Unrelated Individuals
  Forming a Group
  Waiting to Cross